COLLECTORS EDITION

# Slow Cooking

R&R PUBLICATIONS MARKETING PTY LTD

Published by
R&R Publications Marketing Pty Ltd
ABN 78 348 105 138

PO Box 254, Carlton North
Victoria 3054, Australia
PHONE: (61 3) 9381 2199
FAX: (61 3) 9381 2689
E-MAIL: info@randrpublications.com.au
WEBSITE: www.randrpublications.com.au
AUSTRALIA-WIDE TOLL-FREE: 1800 063 296

Slow Cooking – Collectors Edition

PUBLISHER: Anthony Carroll
PRODUCTION MANAGER: Neil Hargreaves
GRAPHIC DESIGNER: Elain Wei Voon Loh
FOOD EDITOR: Neil Hargreaves
FOOD PHOTOGRAPHY: Brent Parker Jones,
R&R Photostudio (www.rrphotostudio.com.au)
FOOD STYLISTS: Lee Blaylock
PROOFREADER: Gabrielle Stefanos

ISBN 978-1-74022-583-0

First Edition Printed February 2008
This Edition Printed March 2009
Computer Typeset in
ITC Avant Garde Gothic
Printed in China

# Contents

# Introduction

All foods, as we know, are prone to seasonal change. This is because our food histories and cultural eating practices usually originate from the land, from the simple beginnings of subsistence farming and peasant cookery. There is, however, another kind of food seasonality – different foods come in and out of favour according to the fashions of the time.

What was in fashion 10 years ago is different from what is in vogue today. The fascinating part of the current change in food perceptions is the return of many of the old ways of cooking. Fast food has definitely been put in its place and a return to slow food is very much back in the public's perception of what is both good for you and what is presentable at the table. Within the idea that some of the old ways of cooking are truly worthy and should be enjoyed alongside quick meals, speedy salads and wok-tossed minute meals, there is a strong place for the slow and hearty fireside foods of old.

The slow-cooking pot that bubbled away for hours on the edge of the fireplace made a successful electronic conversion in the late '60s and early '70s and became the 'crockpot'.

Like most fashions, crockpots were heartily embraced and people realised that an appliance that could slow-cook a wet meal automatically (usually without the need for stirring or watching over) was a convenient way to produce wonderful traditional family meals without being tied to the kitchen for the entire day. The crockpot has, however, like many food innovations become identified with the time of its invention and is now seen as old technology. Ask your mum and she probably still has one stashed in the back of her cupboard somewhere or under the preserving equipment gathering dust in the back shed.

It will likely be beige or burnt orange in colour with a motif on the side – a testament to the time of its previous popularity.

These cookers have recently had a makeover and with the resurgence of interest in slow food and traditional cooking techniques they are perfectly placed to again be seen with pride bubbling away on the side of the kitchen bench, imparting beautiful aromas to your kitchen while happily cooking away unaided and unsupervised.

Traditional slow-cooked soups, continental casseroles, hearty stews and exotic tagines – the traditional and slow foods from all nations – are back on the food agenda and the poetic and provincial idea of slow cooking inexpensive cuts of meat is seen at some of the finest eateries around the Western world.

In short, the slow cooker is back, looking good and ready for service in the modern kitchen.

Once you have started cooking with a slow cooker you will soon realise its convenience and economy. The slow cooker is a low-fuss appliance that is also a low-energy user – once the cooker reaches core temperature the mass of the food helps to retain its own heat and very little extra heat is needed to maintain temperature. Flavours are trapped inside the cooking environment and each component imparts its character and takes on the flavours of what is around it. Good quality stocks, fresh vegetables, citrus rinds and robust flavours such as rosemary and thyme are the winning elements to beautiful old-fashioned cookery.

One of the labour- and time-saving elements of this style of cooking is the fact that you can create the ultimate cooking short cut by cutting up your meats and vegetables and adding them to the one pot (your slow cooker), with the only dishes to wash being your cutting board and knife. The rest is taken care of from cooking to serving, leaving you with only the ceramic insert and the dinner plates for the after-dinner wash-up. There are few simpler and more fundamental ways of cooking.

# Getting to Know Your Slow Cooker

The various makes of slow cookers respond a little differently to each other so you'll need to gauge cooking time for yourself from the first couple of recipes you try out – if your cooker is particularly large or lower powered then you may need to add a little extra cooking time than the recipe indicates.

For the first few recipes mark down your starting and finishing time so that you quickly get a feel for how your particular slow cooker responds. Keep an eye on your slow cooker in the late stages of cooking to see if it requires any more or less cooking time or a top-up of liquid.

Your slow cooker is exactly that and cannot recover heat losses quickly, so lift the lid only when instructed.

If you feel you must remove the lid several times, remember to extend the cooking time a little.

You will learn whether to add extra time by simply looking at your meal in the late stages of cooking.

Due to the unique wraparound heating system, low temperature and long cooking periods, slow cooker temperatures cannot be accurately compared to an oven or a frying pan. So that you can prepare your own favourite recipes in a slow cooker, we have provided a conversion table on page 23.

Cooking settings on most slow cookers are LOW and HIGH. Food will be brought to simmer on all settings. The LOW and HIGH settings determine the time needed to reach a simmer. Avoid sudden temperature changes when using your slow cooker as it will not be able to withstand them. Do not put in frozen or very cold foods if the ceramic bowl has been preheated or is hot to the touch.

The removable ceramic bowl may be used in the oven and is ideal to use when adding a pastry crust to your favourite stews. Be careful not to place the ceramic bowl on the range surface or burners.

Your slow cooker can help you get the best advantage from your freezer.

You can prepare double the usual quantity of a favourite casserole and when cooked, freeze the extra amount. The best way to freeze food for later reheating is to turn it out from the slow cooker after cooking to allow the ceramic insert to cool. Then wash the ceramic insert and coat it with a little oil or butter before returning the cooled food to it. Cover the ceramic insert and freeze until the food is set. Once set, turn out the block of frozen food and transfer it to a large freezer bag. Then when you return the food to the slow cooker for reheating, it will always fit back in perfectly. Do not use the ceramic bowl for storing food in the freezer indefinitely, and always remember that you cannot return frozen foods to a preheated cooker. When you want a slow-cooked meal without any preparation at all, just place the frozen food into the cooker and heat for 5 to 8 hours. The slow, gentle heating from the cooker will not dry out the meal you are reheating.

You can prepare a recipe the night before in the removable ceramic bowl and store it in the refrigerator so that when you are ready to cook the bowl can be transferred to the slow cooker heating base unit. Just make sure that the base unit has not been preheated. Cook on the desired setting, using a little extra time than given in the recipe.

Most vegetables should be cut into small pieces, or at least quartered, and placed near the sides and bottom of your cooker. Carrots and other dense root vegetables should be peeled and put where they will be covered by liquid.

An unusual characteristic of the slow cooker is that meats generally cook faster than most root vegetables. The heating element of the slow cooker runs around the outer edges of the insert and because of this it is a good idea to arrange vegetables towards that area.

Small food portions can be cooked in the slow cooker, but the times will vary. Because there is no direct heat at the bottom always fill the cooker at least half full to conform to the recommended times. Adjust your recipe volume according to the size of your slow cooker.

Roasts can be cooked on low without adding water, but a small amount of water is recommended because the gravies are especially tasty and it would be a shame to leave them behind.

The more fat or marbling the meat has, the less liquid you will need as the natural fats in the food help to baste and moisten the finished food.

Gravy-making can be done right inside your cooker.

**1** Remove the foods from the pot, leaving the juices.

**2** Prepare a smooth paste of about ¼ cup plain flour or cornflour to ¼ cup water.

**3** Pour mixture into the liquid in your cooker and stir well.

**4** Turn to high and cook, stirring occasionally, until mixture thickens and becomes slightly transparent (approximately 15 to 20 minutes). Then it is ready to serve.

Since the liquid content of meats and vegetables will vary, you may end up with a recipe with too much liquid. The excess can be reduced by removing the cover and setting the cooker on high for about 45 minutes. Most recipes cooked in the slow cooker will be juicier since the slow cooking prevents evaporation.

Your slow cooker should never be filled higher than 2cm from the top. If it is too full the lid will lift while the food is cooking.

With the high setting, if by chance your dish of food does dry out, do not simply add cold liquid; it is best to boil the kettle and add some extra water, or if you have extra stock, heat it in a small saucepan before adding to the slow cooker.

It is advisable to generally always preheat your slow cooker for 10 to 15 minutes before use. This helps food come up to cooking temperature faster.

**ADAPTING YOUR FAVOURITE RECIPES FOR THE SLOW COOKER**

Here are a few basic hints which will help when you come to adapt other recipes.

- Allow sufficient cooking time on low setting.

- Follow the conversion guide given on page 23.

- Do not add as much water as conventional recipes indicate.

Remember: in a slow cooker liquids do not 'boil away' as in other methods of cooking, so usually you'll have more liquid at the end of the cooking process instead of less.

Always cook with the cover on. Your slow cooker cooks best if left undisturbed. Lifting the lid can lengthen the cooking time; if you need to stir your dish, do it during the last few hours of cooking time or only when instructed in the recipe.

Generally, 1 to 2 cups of liquid are enough for any recipe unless it contains rice, pasta or other absorbing grains such as polenta, couscous or quinoa. The other exceptions are pot-roast-style dishes where you expect to have liquids at the end and classic Italian styled 'bolito-misto' dishes where you boil and simmer meats and discard the cooking liquid at the end of the cooking process. In the case of the pot roast, any vegetables and the main joint of meat can be lifted out at the end of its cooking time with a slotted spoon and tongs. Then, with the addition of thirsty grains such as those mentioned above, thick and wet rustic-style gruels can be made to form a magnificent base for a truly old-fashioned meal – simply turn the cooker to high, add some grains and cook for 45 minutes with the lid removed (while the main meat is rested and carved).

Slow cooking is one-step cooking – many steps in conventional recipes may be deleted. You can add all ingredients to the slow cooker at one time and cook for approximately 8 hours.

There are three important exceptions: milk, sour cream and fresh cream should be added during the last half hour of cooking.

When cooking with herbs and spices, whole herbs and spices are preferable. When a recipe calls for dried beans, the beans should be soaked overnight, then cooked on high for 2 to 3 hours. Or you can cook them overnight on low with water and 1 small teaspoon of bicarbonate of soda added to speed up the breakdown of the beans. Instead of soaking or cooking overnight, they may also be parboiled first.

Do not precook seafood or frozen vegetables; just rinse and drain thoroughly before adding to other ingredients. These foods cook quickly, so it is best to add them during the last hour of cooking.

When a crisp topping of crumbs or grated cheese is called for, transfer food from the slow cooker to a platter and brown it either with a torch or in the oven. The removable bowls with some models are versatile, as they can be easily put in the oven to achieve the desired topping.

Dumplings may be cooked in broth or gravy on high. Drop the mixture by spoonfuls into a simmering stew or liquid and cook covered for about 30 minutes on high.

If cooked rice is called for, stir raw rice in with other ingredients. Add 1 cup of extra liquid per cup of raw rice. Use long-grain rice for best results in all-day cooking.

Some foods do not benefit from slow cooking, so do not use any of the following unless the recipe says so:

- Crisp-cooked green vegetables

- Noodles

- Macaroni

- Asian vegetables

- Puddings or sauces made with a foundation of milk or cream

Although these foods are familiar favourites, care must be taken when using them in slow cooker recipes.

You can cook without liquid. For example, fish and sausages can be placed in the cooker, covered, and cooked for 2 to 4 hours, depending on the thickness of the meat. Or, you scrub and dry new potatoes and arrange them in the cooker, cover, and cook for 8 to 10 hours.

**GET INVENTIVE**

With the guidelines in this introduction you should be able to take any appropriate recipe and convert it to a slow-cooking recipe.

Think outside the square and make the slow cooker work for you. Anything from a hearty porridge with dried fruit slowly cooked overnight to feed a family when it rises for a chilly winter breakfast or preparing a late sweet snack that cooks away as you settle in front of the evening television after the main meal – the applications and variations are virtually unlimited.

**COOKING TIME CONVERSION GUIDE**

| OVEN OR STOVETOP COOKING TIME | SLOW COOKER LOW COOKING TIME | SLOW COOKER HIGH COOKING TIME |
| --- | --- | --- |
| 15–30 mins | 4–6 hrs | 1½–2½ hrs |
| 35–45 mins | 6–8 hrs | 3–4 hrs |
| 50 mins–3 hrs | 8–12 hrs | 4–6 hrs |

This guide applies particularly to casseroles. Most meat and vegetable combinations will require at least 7 hours on low.

## TYPES OF COOKERS

All of the slow cookers on the market vary in shape, size and volume capacity. When choosing one there are many considerations to ponder.

All cookers consume approximately the same amount of power.

The settings vary according to the make and size and individual style of each cooker, so if you are buying a new cooker, choose wisely and consider your potential end needs.

You can buy cookers with ceramic containers permanently fixed into the outer casings, where the heating elements are placed between the outer casing and the cooking pot. Some of these styles come with detachable power cords so that the entire unit can be taken to the table to serve from.

Another style of cooker has a removable inner ceramic cooking container, which means that only the cooking pot is taken to the table. This style of slow cooker enables food to be easily browned or crisped under the grill for final presentation.

In these cookers the heating elements are fitted within the walls of the base unit that the ceramic container fits into.

There are different capacity cookers that vary from 1.5 to 5.5 litres. While the little cookers seem kind of nifty and compact, it is best to get the largest size that you think you can use – once you become familiar with this appliance you will see the benefit of cooking double quantities and large joints of meat. It allows for greater versatility and is an easy way to feed a large amount of guests.

## HOW TO CLEAN AND CARE FOR YOUR SLOW COOKER

Never submerge the slow cooker cooking unit in water. Remove the ceramic bowl and place the bowl in the dishwasher or wash with hot soapy water as soon as possible after emptying it.

Do not pour in cold water if the ceramic bowl is hot. When cleaning your slow cooker do not use abrasive cleaning compounds. A cloth, sponge or rubber spatula will usually remove the residue. If necessary, a plastic cleaning pad may be used.

The metal liner may be cleaned with a damp cloth or scouring pad, or sprayed lightly with an all-purpose cleaner to maintain.

To remove water spots and other stains, use a non-abrasive cleaner or vinegar.

The outside of the slow cooker may be cleaned with soft cloth and warm soapy water and wiped dry. Do not use abrasive cleaners on the outside.

Care should be taken to avoid hitting the ceramic pot with metal spoons or water taps. Do not put frozen or very cold foods in the slow cooker if the unit has been preheated or is hot to the touch.

## SAFETY

When using electrical kitchen appliances, basic safety precautions should always be followed.

Read all instructions and become thoroughly familiar with your slow cooker.

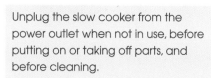

Do not touch hot surfaces; always use handles or knobs.

Caution must be used when moving the slow cooker if it contains hot oil or other hot liquids.

Unplug the slow cooker from the power outlet when not in use, before putting on or taking off parts, and before cleaning.

Close supervision is necessary when the slow cooker is used by or near children.

Use your slow cooker on an even and stable surface.

Do not place slow cooker units on or near a hot gas or electric burner, or in a heated oven. Only the ceramic inserts should be placed in the oven or under a grill.

# Remember the
## three basic rules...

- **SIGHT:** Does it look ready? Does it need a little more liquid?

- **TEXTURE:** Test with a fork and see if it easily pierces the meat and vegetables.

- **TASTE:** The best final test is always to taste the food in your slow cooker and see if it tastes ready for the table.

Hearty root vegetables and robust herbs – making a slow soup is the best way to enjoy a nourishing meal in a bowl. Choose your favourite vegetables and stock, then season and cook until falling apart. It can be that simple. To turn your soup into something special remove any coarse herbs such as rosemary, thyme or bay leaves, use a hand-held blender to liquefy the soup, return the herbs then add a joint of meat and cook until tender, before flaking the meat off the bone and serving. This will take hours, but that is the true joy of capturing and developing flavours in your slow cooker.

# Soups

COLLECTORS EDITION

# Soups

COLLECTORS EDITION

# Portuguese Potato and Bean Soup

serves 6–8

**PREPARATION** 15 mins   **COOKING** 4 hrs 30 mins

4 cloves garlic, crushed

2 medium onions, diced

2 medium carrots, diced

4 medium desiree potatoes, diced

1 green capsicum, finely diced

425g canned Roma tomatoes, finely diced

½ medium green cabbage, shredded

425g canned red kidney beans, drained, rinsed

455g smoked Polish sausage, diced

6½ cups chicken stock

salt and freshly ground black pepper

2 tablespoons chopped fresh parsley to garnish

1  Place all the ingredients in a slow cooker on high.

2  Simmer for 4½ hours. Add salt and pepper to taste and serve piping hot, garnished with parsley.

**NOTE** You'll love the flavours in this satisfying soup. It's incredibly easy to prepare, and since it contains no oil you can make it a regular, guilt-free indulgence.

German Potato Soup with Cauliflower and Caraway

serves 6

# German Potato Soup with Cauliflower and Caraway

**PREPARATION** 20 mins   **COOKING** 3 hrs 35 mins

1 bunch spring onions

2 tablespoons olive oil

1 medium cauliflower head, cut into florets (reserve small florets)

600g desiree potatoes, peeled, diced

1 teaspoon caraway seeds, plus extra for garnish

6 cups vegetable stock

2 tablespoons natural yoghurt

1   Cut 5cm lengths off the end of each spring onion. Using a sharp knife, slice these into thin strips, keeping one end intact to hold the strips together. Plunge the strips into a bowl of iced water and set aside until they curl (about 1 hour). Slice the remaining spring onion.

2   Then heat the olive oil in a slow cooker on a high setting and add the remaining spring onion and the cauliflower florets, potatoes and caraway seeds and cook for 50 minutes.

3   Add the stock and bring the soup to the simmer for 2 hours, then process with a food processor or hand-held blender until smooth. Add the reserved small cauliflower florets and simmer for 45 minutes. Serve the soup with a dollop of yoghurt, a sprinkling of caraway seeds and the spring onion curls.

Porcini Mushroom Soup

serves 6

# Porcini Mushroom Soup

**PREPARATION** 10 mins   **COOKING** 2 hrs 40 mins

15g dried porcini mushrooms

½ cup boiling water

2 tablespoons olive oil

2 cloves garlic, crushed

1 leek, sliced

6 French shallots, chopped

285g white mushrooms, thinly sliced

500g forest mushrooms, including shiitake, oyster and Swiss brown, thinly sliced

2 tablespoons plain flour

4 cups good quality chicken, beef or vegetable stock

1 cup double cream

½ bunch fresh flat-leaf parsley, chopped

30 fresh basil leaves, shredded

1 tablespoon fresh oregano

salt and freshly ground black pepper

ground nutmeg

1  Add the dried porcini mushrooms to the boiling water and set aside. When the mushrooms have softened, remove them from the liquid and set aside. Strain the mushroom liquid through a muslin-lined sieve to separate sand and grit, and reserve the liquid.

2  Heat the olive oil in a large saucepan and add the garlic, leeks and shallots and cook until golden (about 3 minutes). Add all the fresh mushrooms and cook over a very high heat until the mushrooms soften and their liquid evaporates (about 7 minutes). Reserve a few mushroom pieces for the garnish.

3  Transfer the leek and mushroom mixture to a preheated slow cooker set on high, then sprinkle with the flour and stir well to enable the flour to be absorbed. Add the stock and the porcini mushrooms together with the reserved liquid. Stir to combine. Cook for 2 hours.

4  Add the cream, then turn to low and cook for a further 30 minutes or until slightly thickened. Add half the parsley and the basil and oregano and season to taste with salt and freshly ground black pepper. To serve, ladle into individual bowls sprinkle with extra parsley, reserved mushrooms, some nutmeg and a small dollop of extra cream if desired.

serves 4

# Roma Tomato, Lentil and Basil Soup

**PREPARATION** 30 mins   **COOKING** 2 hrs 40 mins

½ cup brown lentils

1 kg Roma tomatoes

2 onions, diced

2 tablespoons sun-dried tomato purée

3 cups vegetable stock

1 bay leaf

freshly ground black pepper

3 tablespoons chopped fresh basil, plus extra leaves to garnish

1 Rinse the lentils, drain and add them to a large saucepan of boiling water. Simmer, covered, for 25 minutes or until tender. Drain, rinse and set aside.

2 Meanwhile, place the tomatoes in a bowl, cover with boiling water, leave for 30 seconds, then drain. Remove the skins, deseed and chop.

3 In a slow cooker on high, add the onions and stir in the tomatoes, tomato purée, stock, bay leaf and pepper. Cover and bring to the simmer. Simmer for 2¼ hours.

4 Remove and discard the bay leaf, then purée the soup until smooth in a food processor or with a hand-held blender. Stir in the lentils and chopped basil, then reheat. Serve garnished with the fresh basil leaves.

Spanish Pea Soup

# Spanish Pea Soup

**PREPARATION** 10 mins plus 1 hr standing   **COOKING** 4 hrs 45 mins

2 cups dried green split peas, rinsed

3 cups water

1 tablespoon olive oil

1 tablespoon Spanish paprika

2 cups diced onion

1 clove garlic, crushed

1 cup chopped green capsicum

¾ cup thinly sliced carrot

3 medium red potatoes, peeled, cubed

7 cups chicken or vegetable stock

salt and freshly ground black pepper

420g canned sweet corn

½ bunch fresh chives, chopped to garnish

1   Place split peas in a large pot, cover with the water and bring to the boil. Simmer for 2 minutes then remove from the heat and cover. Let stand for 1 hour.

2   Heat the oil in a large saucepan and add the Spanish paprika, onion and garlic and sauté for 5 minutes until the mixture is fragrant and the onions have softened.

3   Add the green capsicum, carrot and potato. Toss the vegetables thoroughly with the onion mixture until well coated, then continue to cook for 10 minutes, stirring thoroughly during the cooking.

4   Transfer to a slow cooker set on high and add the stock, split peas and salt and pepper to taste. Cook for 4 hours or until the split peas are very tender.

5   Reserve ½ cup of corn, then add the remainder to the soup and purée the soup until thick and smooth. Return the soup to the slow cooker and cook for a further 30 minutes. Serve scattered with a few corn kernels and some chopped chives on top.

serves 6

# Chicken and Leek Soup with Herb Dumplings

PREPARATION 30 mins   COOKING 5 hrs

4 chicken cutlets

1 onion, chopped

1 carrot, chopped

herb bundle made up of

fresh tarragon, parsley and

a bay leaf

6 cups hot water

60g butter

300g potatoes, peeled,

diced

3 large leeks, sliced

salt and freshly ground

black pepper

2 boneless skinless chicken

breasts, cut into small pieces

2 teaspoons chopped fresh

tarragon

145mL light cream

salt and freshly ground

black pepper

⅓ cup water

## DUMPLINGS

125g plain flour

½ teaspoon bicarbonate

of soda

30g fresh white breadcrumbs

50g butter

3 tablespoons chopped

fresh herbs, such as tarragon,

parsley or chives

1  Place the chicken, onion, carrot and bundle of herbs in a slow cooker with the hot water. Cover and cook for 2 hours on high, then strain the stock and skim off any fat. Finely chop the chicken, discarding the skin and bones.

2  Heat half of the butter in a large saucepan, add the potatoes and two-thirds of the leeks, cover and cook for 10 minutes. Transfer to the slow cooker and add 4 cups of the stock and season. Cook for 50 minutes, until vegetables have softened. Blend in a food processor or with a hand-held blender until smooth, return to the slow cooker, then stir in the cooked chicken.

3  Add the rest of the butter and the chicken breast and the remaining leek. Cook for 2 hours, adding more stock if necessary. Remove from the heat and stir in the fresh tarragon and cream. To serve, divide between 6 bowls, drain the dumplings and add 2 to each bowl.

**DUMPLINGS** (make while finishing the soup)

1  Mix together the flour, bicarbonate of soda, breadcrumbs, butter, herbs and seasoning. Stir in water, then shape into 12 dumplings. Cook in simmering salted water for 15 minutes.

serves 8

# Sienese Bean Soup

**PREPARATION** 10 mins plus 12 hrs soaking   **COOKING** 3 hrs 40 mins

200g dried red kidney beans, soaked overnight

1 cup vegetable stock

3 cups water

¼ cup olive oil

2 carrots, diced

2 sticks celery, sliced

3 zucchini, sliced

425g canned crushed tomatoes

½ cup dry white wine

3 cloves garlic, crushed

2 bay leaves

8 cups chicken stock

250g cabbage, sliced

2 tablespoons chopped fresh basil

2 tablespoons chopped fresh parsley

freshly ground black pepper

1 Drain beans, put in a saucepan and add vegetable stock and water. Bring to the boil and boil vigorously for 10 minutes. Lower heat and simmer for 1 hour.

2 Meanwhile, in a slow cooker set on high, add oil, carrots, celery, zucchini, tomatoes, wine, garlic and bay leaves and cook for 1 hour.

3 Drain the red kidney beans and add to slow cooker with chicken stock. Cook for a further 2 hours.

4 Add cabbage and cook for 30 minutes more. Serve topped with chopped basil and parsley and cracked black pepper.

serves 6–8

# Savoury Pumpkin Soup

**PREPARATION** 15 mins   **COOKING** 6 hrs 45 mins

1 kg pumpkin, peeled, diced

400mL canned tomato juice

1 tablespoon raw sugar

8 cups water

salt and freshly ground

black pepper

1 bay leaf

few drops of Tabasco sauce

2 chicken stock cubes

½ cup pouring cream

2 tablespoons chopped

fresh parsley

1  With the exception of parsley and cream, combine all ingredients in a slow cooker and cook for 6½ hours on low.

2  Remove bay leaf. Process the mixture a cupful at a time in a food processor.

3  Return mixture to slow cooker and reheat for 15 minutes. Add cream and allow to warm through.

4  Serve sprinkled with fresh parsley.

Roasted Tomato, Red Capsicum and Bread Soup

serves 4

# Roasted Tomato, Red Capsicum and Bread Soup

**PREPARATION** 10 mins   **COOKING** 3 hrs 10 mins

2 tablespoons olive oil

1 kg Roma tomatoes

2 red capsicums

3 cloves garlic, crushed

2 onions, finely diced

2 teaspoons ground cumin

1 teaspoon ground coriander

4 cups chicken stock

2 slices white bread, crusts removed and torn into pieces

1 tablespoon balsamic vinegar

salt and freshly ground black pepper

1   Lightly oil a baking dish, place tomatoes and capsicums in the dish and bake in a moderate oven for 20 minutes (or until the skins have blistered). After 15 minutes add the garlic, onion, cumin and coriander for the last 5 minutes. Set aside to cool, then remove the tomatoes and capsicums, take off their skins and roughly chop.

2   Heat a slow cooker on a high setting and add all of the mixture from the bottom of the baking dish. Add tomatoes, capsicums and stock and cook for 2 hours. Add bread, balsamic vinegar and salt and pepper, and cook for a further 50 minutes.

Indian Spiced Potato and Onion Soup

serves 4

# Indian Spiced Potato and Onion Soup

**PREPARATION** 10 mins   **COOKING** 3 hrs 15 mins

1 tablespoon vegetable oil

1 onion, finely chopped

1cm piece fresh ginger, peeled, finely diced

2 large potatoes, cut into 1cm pieces

2 teaspoons ground cumin

2 teaspoons ground coriander

½ teaspoon ground turmeric

1 teaspoon ground cinnamon

2 tablespoons cold water

4 cups chicken stock

salt and freshly ground black pepper

1 tablespoon natural yoghurt to garnish

1   Heat the oil in a large saucepan. Cook onion and ginger for 5 minutes or until softened. Add the potatoes and cook for another 5 minutes, stirring often.

2   Mix the cumin, coriander, turmeric and cinnamon with cold water to make a paste. Add to the onion and potatoes and fry for 2 minutes, stirring well to release flavours.

3   Transfer the potato and spice mixture to a heated slow cooker set on a high setting. Add the stock and season to taste. Bring to the simmer and cover, then cook for 3 hours or until the potato is tender. Blend until smooth in a food processor or with a hand-held blender. Return to the slow cooker and heat through, then adjusting the seasoning again. Serve garnished with the yoghurt and more pepper.

**NOTE** This delicately spiced soup makes a great start to an Indian meal. It also makes a satisfying snack on its own, served with warm naan bread and a salad.

# Sweet Potato and Rosemary Soup

**PREPARATION** 20 mins  **COOKING** 5 hrs 15 mins

2 tablespoons olive oil

2 cloves garlic, crushed

1 medium onion, chopped

3 tablespoons chopped fresh rosemary

2 tablespoons puréed semi-dried tomato

1 medium carrot, sliced

1 large potato, sliced

700g sweet potato, sliced

4 cups chicken stock

salt and freshly ground black pepper

1  Heat the oil in a saucepan, add the garlic, onion and one-third of the rosemary, and cook on a medium heat for 5 minutes. Add the semi-dried tomato purée and cook for 1 minute.

2  Add the carrot, potato and sweet potato, and cook for a further 6 minutes.

3  Transfer to slow cooker set on high and add the stock and salt and pepper. Cook for 5 hours, or until the vegetables are soft.

4  Purée the soup in a food processor, then return to the slow cooker. Add the remaining rosemary and heat through before serving.

Seafood is probably the fastest food to prepare in a slow cooker, but the flavours still develop magnificently. Tougher seafoods that are normally fast-grilled are perfect for the slow cooker because they break down and become subtle to the bite while retaining the flavours of the sea – calamari and squid work perfectly. Whole deep-sea fish stuffed with citrus and herbs also cook magnificently in a hearty broth or chilli-laden concoction. Prepare your stocks and vegetables and start to cook them before adding fish or shellfish.

# Seafood

COLLECTORS EDITION

# Seafood

COLLECTORS EDITION

| # Seafood Casserole

**PREPARATION** 5 mins  **COOKING** 2 hrs

1 tablespoon olive oil

1 medium onion, roughly chopped

1 leek, finely chopped

2 cloves garlic, crushed

2 cups canned tomatoes

2 bay leaves

1 tablespoon chopped fresh parsley

¼ cup dry white wine

salt and freshly ground black pepper

1 kg assorted fish and seafood*

2 tablespoons chopped fresh oregano to garnish

1  Heat the oil in a frying pan, add onion, leek and garlic and cook for 5 minutes until softened.

2  Transfer to a slow cooker set on high and add the tomatoes, bay leaves, parsley, wine, salt and pepper. Bring to the simmer, cover and cook for 50 minutes.

3  Stir in any firm-fleshed fish and cook for 25 minutes.

4  Stir in the soft-fleshed fish, placing the shellfish on the top. Cover with a lid and continue cooking for 40 minutes (until the fish is tender).

5  Serve garnished with the oregano.

*Suitable fish and seafood include red mullet, monkfish, sea bream, cod, calamari, mussels, shelled prawns and clams.

Bouillabaisse

serves 6

# Bouillabaisse

**PREPARATION** 40 mins   **COOKING** 4 hrs

3 kg mixed fish and seafood,
including firm white fish fillets,
prawns, mussels, crab and
calamari rings

¼ cup olive oil

2 cloves garlic, crushed

2 large onions, chopped

2 leeks, sliced

2 x 400g canned tomatoes

⅔ cup fish stock

1 tablespoon chopped
fresh thyme or 1 teaspoon
dried thyme

2 tablespoons chopped
fresh basil or 1½ teaspoons
dried basil

2 tablespoons chopped
fresh parsley

2 bay leaves

2 tablespoons finely grated
orange rind

1 teaspoon saffron threads

⅔ cup dry white wine

freshly ground black pepper

1   Remove the bones and skin from the fish
fillets and cut into 2cm cubes. Peel and devein
the prawns, leaving the tails intact. Scrub and
remove the beards from the mussels. Cut the
crab into quarters. Set aside.

2   Heat a slow cooker on a high setting, then
add the oil, garlic, onions, leeks, tomatoes and
stock and cook for 1½ hours. Add the thyme,
basil, parsley, bay leaves, orange rind, saffron
and wine. Cook for 30 minutes.

3   Add the fish and crab and cook for 1 hour.
Add the remaining seafood and cook for
1 hour longer or until all fish and seafood are
cooked. Season to taste with black pepper.

Braised Fish with Lemon

serves 4

# Braised Fish
# with Lemon

**PREPARATION** 10 mins   **COOKING** 1 hr 10 mins

2 whole pearl perch or bream

salt and freshly ground

black pepper

1 tomato, sliced

2 lemons, sliced

olive oil

50g butter

fresh parsley leaves to garnish

1  Remove heads from fish, then scale and clean well. Season cavities with salt and pepper, and place slices of tomato and lemon in each cavity. Grease bowl of a slow cooker with olive oil. Place fish in the slow cooker, side by side, and season with salt and pepper. Top with 2 slices of lemon per fish and a drizzle of olive oil. Cover and cook on low for 1 hour.

2  Just before serving cut the butter into small cubes and scatter over the top of each piece of fish before covering again. After 10 minutes carefully remove the fish with a large spatula and arrange on a hot serving dish.

3  Pour the remaining liquid from the slow cooker over the fish. Garnish with a scattering of fresh parsley leaves.

Slow Fish Stew on Rosemary Mash

serves 4

# Slow Fish Stew on Rosemary Mash

**PREPARATION** 20 mins   **COOKING** 3 hrs 10 mins

2 teaspoons olive oil

1 leek, diced, washed

1 clove garlic, crushed

1 teaspoon dried oregano

4 field mushrooms, sliced

1 stick celery, sliced

2 cups canned no-added-salt
diced tomatoes

2 zucchini, sliced

½ cup dry white wine

1 tablespoon no-added-salt
tomato paste

600g firm white fish fillets (such
as ling, flake or blue-eye)

1 tablespoon chopped
fresh basil

1 tablespoon chopped
fresh parsley

## ROSEMARY MASH

1 sprig fresh rosemary

2 teaspoons olive oil

2 large potatoes, peeled,
quartered

¼ cup low-fat milk, warmed

ground white pepper

1   To make the rosemary mash, remove the leaves from the rosemary sprig. Place the leaves and the oil in a small saucepan over a low heat and heat until warm. Remove the pan from the heat and set aside to allow the flavours to develop. If possible, do this several hours in advance; the longer the leaves steep in the oil, the more pronounced the flavour becomes. Boil potatoes until tender. Drain well. Add milk and rosemary oil. Mash the potatoes and season with white pepper.

2   Meanwhile, heat a slow cooker on high. Add the oil, leek, garlic, oregano, mushrooms, celery, zucchini, tomatoes and wine. Cook for 40 minutes.

3   Stir in the tomato paste. Cook for 30 minutes or until the mixture starts to thicken.

4   Reduce the heat to low and add the fish. Cook for 2 hours until the fish is just cooked; take care not to overcook or the fish will fall apart. Stir in the basil and parsley. Serve with the mash.

Ling with Brown Butter Sauce

serves 6

# Ling with Brown Butter Sauce

**PREPARATION** 5 mins   **COOKING** 2 hrs 30 mins

1 kg ling

3 teaspoons salt

1 tablespoon white wine vinegar

1 bay leaf

1 onion, sliced

4 whole black peppercorns

few stalks of parsley

grated rind of 1 lemon

2 tablespoons chopped fresh dill

1 tablespoon capers

**BROWN BUTTER SAUCE**

60g butter

2 tablespoons white wine vinegar

1  Wash the fish and cut into serving pieces.

2  Place in a slow cooker and cover with cold water. Add salt, white wine vinegar, bay leaf, onion and peppercorns and cook for 2 hours and 20 minutes on low.

3  Lift with a fish slice onto a cutting board. Scrape away the skin from both sides and carefully remove larger bones. Transfer to a heated serving dish and keep hot while making the sauce. Sprinkle parsley, lemon rind, dill and capers over fish.

4  To make the sauce, heat a small frying pan, add the butter and heat carefully until it begins to turn brown, being careful not to burn it. Pour over ling. Add the white wine vinegar to pan and reduce by half – this only takes a second. Pour over fish as well and serve immediately with lemon wedges.

Shellfish Stew

serves 6

# Shellfish Stew

PREPARATION 35 mins   COOKING 1 hr 25 mins

750g live lobster or 2 frozen lobster tails

6 tablespoons olive oil

500g prawns, shelled

500g cod or other firm-fleshed fish steak, cut into bite-size pieces

250g whole small calamari, cleaned

1 small onion, chopped

1 red capsicum, chopped

3 cloves garlic, crushed

3 medium tomatoes, peeled, deseeded, chopped

¼ teaspoon saffron threads

2 tablespoons minced parsley

1 bay leaf

½ teaspoon dried thyme

¼ teaspoon chilli flakes

¾ cup dry white wine

¼ cup lemon juice

salt and freshly ground black pepper

12 very small clams, thoroughly scrubbed

12 mussels, scrubbed, de-bearded

1   As close as possible to the time you are going to cook the lobster, have the fishmonger cut the claws and tail from it and break them into serving-size pieces.

2   Heat the oil in a large frying pan and quickly sauté lobster over high heat for 3 minutes. Remove and set aside.

3   In the frying pan on a medium heat cook the prawns and fish for 3½ minutes. Remove and set aside.

4   Add calamari, onion, capsicum and garlic and cook for 3½ minutes. Transfer mixture to a slow cooker set on high and stir in tomatoes, saffron, parsley, bay leaf, thyme and chilli flakes and cook for 25 minutes. Stir in wine, lemon juice and salt and pepper and cook for 20 minutes. Add reserved seafood, cover and simmer for 30 minutes longer.

5   Meanwhile, in a covered pan, steam clams and mussels with 2 cups of water over high heat. As clams and mussels open, remove them and add to casserole. Serve immediately.

Kedgeree

serves 4

# Kedgeree

**PREPARATION** 10 mins   **COOKING** 2 hrs 10 mins

500g smoked trout or cod

1 leek, diced, washed

30g butter

1 onion, finely sliced

1 teaspoon curry powder

1 cup basmati rice

2 cups boiling water

1 sachet Japanese dashi stock

2 tablespoons cream

2 hard-boiled eggs, coarsely chopped

freshly ground black pepper

2 tablespoons chopped fresh parsley

1  Place smoked fish in saucepan, cover with cold water and bring slowly to the simmer. Cook for 6 minutes, drain and flake.

2  Melt butter in a large frying pan over a medium heat and fry onion until soft. Add curry powder and cook, stirring, for 2 minutes. Add rice and leeks and fry gently for 5 minutes, stirring, until rice is translucent yet slightly brown in colour.

3  Place rice mixture in a slow cooker and add boiling water, dashi stock and flaked fish. Gently stir to combine all ingredients, cover and cook on high for 2 hours.

4  When ready to serve add cream and eggs and toss gently with a fork. Season to taste with freshly ground black pepper. Sprinkle with parsley. Serve with lemon wedges if desired.

Sour Prawn Curry

serves 4

# Sour Prawn Curry

**PREPARATION** 15 mins   **COOKING** 1 hr 45 mins

2 cups coconut milk

1 teaspoon shrimp paste

2 tablespoons Thai green curry paste

1 stalk lemongrass, finely chopped or ½ teaspoon dried lemongrass, soaked in hot water until soft

2 fresh green chillies, chopped

1 tablespoon ground cumin

1 tablespoon ground coriander

500g large uncooked prawns, shelled, deveined (leaving tails intact)

3 cucumbers, halved and sliced

115g canned bamboo shoots, drained

1 tablespoon tamarind concentrate, dissolved in 3 tablespoons hot water

1  Place the coconut milk, shrimp paste, curry paste, lemongrass, chillies, cumin and coriander in a slow cooker set on high and bring to a simmer. Stirring occasionally, cook for 1 hour.

2  Stir the prawns, cucumbers, bamboo shoots and tamarind mixture into the coconut milk mixture and cook, stirring occasionally, for 45 minutes or until the prawns are cooked.

3  Serve with steamed rice.

serves 4

# Creole Prawns

**PREPARATION** 25 mins   **COOKING** 3 hrs 35 mins

1 tablespoon olive oil

1 large onion, diced

1 clove garlic, crushed

1 small green capsicum, diced

3 sticks celery, diced

1 cup tomato pasta sauce

400g canned whole peeled

tomatoes

1 teaspoon smoked paprika

1 teaspoon salt

¼ teaspoon black pepper

grated rind of 1 lemon

500g uncooked king prawns,

shelled, deveined

(leaving tails intact)

1  Heat the oil in a large frying pan. Add
the onion and cook over a medium heat
for 2 minutes. Add the garlic and cook for
a further minute, stirring constantly.

2  Combine onion and garlic and all
ingredients, except prawns, in a slow
cooker and cook on high for 2½ hours.

3  Add the prawns, stir and reduce heat.
Continue to cook on low for another hour.

Goan-Style Fish and Coconut Curry

serves 4

# Goan-Style Fish and Coconut Curry

**PREPARATION** 20 mins   **COOKING** 1 hr 20 mins

2 tomatoes

2 cardamom pods, bruised

1 teaspoon ground coriander

1 teaspoon ground cumin

1 teaspoon ground cinnamon

1 teaspoon hot chilli powder

½ teaspoon ground turmeric

2 tablespoons water

2 tablespoons vegetable oil

1 onion, finely chopped

1 clove garlic, finely chopped

25mm piece fresh root ginger, finely chopped

400mL coconut milk

700g skinless white fish fillet, such as haddock or cod, cut into 25mm chunks

salt to taste

fresh coriander leaves to garnish

1   Place tomatoes in a bowl, cover with boiling water and leave to stand for 30 seconds. Peel, then finely chop.

2   Crush cardamom seeds using a mortar and pestle. Add coriander, cumin, cinnamon, chilli powder, turmeric and water and mix to a paste. Set aside.

3   Heat oil in a large heavy-based saucepan. Cook onion, garlic and ginger for 3 minutes or until softened. Add spice paste, mix well and cook for 1 minute, stirring constantly.

4   Transfer to a slow cooker on a high setting, pour in coconut milk and bring to the simmer for 30 minutes. Add fish, tomatoes and salt. Partly cover and cook for a further 45 minutes or until fish turns opaque and is cooked through. Garnish with coriander leaves and serve on a bed of rice.

| # Slowfood Paella

**PREPARATION** 25 mins   **COOKING** 2 hrs 45 mins

500g firm white fish fillets, chopped

285g peeled uncooked prawns

200g scallops

3 calamari, cleaned, sliced

1 tablespoon chopped fresh parsley

1 tablespoon olive oil

2 onions, chopped

2 cloves garlic, crushed

1 tablespoon fresh thyme leaves

2 teaspoons finely grated lemon rind

4 ripe tomatoes, chopped

2½ cups short-grain white rice

pinch saffron threads, soaked in 2 cups water

5 cups chicken or fish stock

300g fresh or frozen peas

2 red capsicums, chopped

1 kg mussels, scrubbed, de-bearded

1　Preheat slow cooker to a high heat level. Add the oil and the onions and stir, then add the garlic, thyme, lemon rind and tomatoes and cook for 15 minutes.

2　Add the rice and saffron mixture and warmed stock. Simmer, stirring occasionally, for 1½ hours or until the rice has absorbed almost all the liquid.

3　Stir in the peas, capsicums and mussels and cook for 20 minutes. Add the fish, prawns and scallops and cook for 20 minutes. Stir in the calamari and parsley and cook for 20 minutes longer or until the seafood is cooked.

Chicken and game birds are a great food to prepare slowly. Whole birds or large pieces on the bone benefit enormously from slow cooking as poultry becomes rich and silky in texture when cooked for many hours. Chicken breasts gently poached in sauces and stocks swimming with fresh seasonal vegetables conjure up memories of elegant restaurant meals. Sophisticated, slowly cooked meals with deeply developed flavours can be easily created at home in a slow cooker that bubbles away while you attend to a busy lifestyle.

# Poultry

COLLECTORS EDITION

# Poultry

COLLECTORS EDITION

# Spanish Chicken with Chorizo

serves 4

**PREPARATION** 15 mins   **COOKING** 5 hrs 45 mins

8 chicken drumsticks

2 tablespoons olive oil

1 onion, sliced

2 cloves garlic, crushed

1 red capsicum, sliced

1 yellow capsicum, sliced

2 teaspoons paprika

3 tablespoons dry sherry

or dry vermouth

2 cups canned chopped

tomatoes

1 bay leaf

1 strip orange rind

2 chorizo sausages, sliced

⅓ cup pitted black olives

salt and freshly ground

black pepper

1   Place the chicken in a large non-stick frying pan and cook without oil for 12 minutes, turning occasionally, until golden. Remove the chicken and set aside. Drain any fat from the pan and discard.

2   Add the oil to the pan and cook the onion, garlic and capsicums for 3 minutes, until softened.

3   Transfer the mixture to a slow cooker set on low, add the chicken and the paprika, sherry or vermouth, tomatoes, bay leaf and orange rind. Bring to temperature and cook for 5 hours.

4   Add the chorizo and olives and cook for a further 30 minutes, then season.

**NOTE** Packed with Mediterranean flavours, this casserole is equally good with rice or crusty bread. You can use stock or orange juice instead of the sherry or vermouth.

Chicken Curry with Jasmine Rice

serves 4

# Chicken Curry with Jasmine Rice

**PREPARATION** 15 mins   **COOKING** 2 hrs 40 mins

2 cups reduced-fat coconut milk

1 cup reduced-salt chicken stock

2 tablespoons green curry paste

3 kaffir lime leaves, shredded

200g chopped pumpkin

4 skinless chicken breast fillets, diced

115g canned bamboo shoots, drained

100g snake beans, chopped

200g broccoli, cut into florets

1 tablespoon fish sauce

1 tablespoon grated palm sugar

2 tablespoons torn fresh Thai basil leaves

## JASMINE RICE

1½ cups jasmine rice

2 stalks lemongrass, halved

4 cups water

1  Combine coconut milk, stock, curry paste and lime leaves in a slow cooker on high. Cook until the sauce begins to thicken. Add the pumpkin and cook for 20 minutes or until it starts to soften.

2  Add the chicken and bamboo shoots and cook for 1 hour. Add the beans, broccoli, fish sauce and palm sugar and cook until the vegetables are tender, for approximately 1 more hour. Then stir through the basil leaves.

3  Meanwhile, to make the jasmine rice, put the rice, lemongrass and water in a pot. Bring to boil and cook over a high heat until steam holes appear in the top of the rice. Reduce the heat to low, cover and cook for 10 minutes or until all the liquid is absorbed and the rice is tender. Transfer the rice to bowls, spoon over the curry and serve.

serves 6

# Chicken Mexico

**PREPARATION** 15 mins   **COOKING** 7 hrs 50 mins

1.5 kg whole chicken

40g butter

2 tablespoons olive oil

2 large onions, sliced

2 cloves garlic, crushed

1 green capsicum, sliced

1 red chilli, diced

1 teaspoon dill seeds

200g canned tomatoes

2 tablespoons tomato paste

150mL chicken stock

2 ears fresh corn, corn cut from the cob

4 tablespoons sour cream

1 tablespoon chopped fresh parsley

1   In a slow cooker on a low heat setting mix all ingredients except the sour cream and parsley. Cook for 7½ hours.

2   Carefully transfer chicken to a serving dish and keep warm. Meanwhile, turn the slow cooker onto high. Simmer the sauce for 20 minutes, add the sour cream and the parsley and pour over the chicken. Serve with rice.

Fricasséed Chicken with Vinegar

serves 4

# Fricasséed Chicken with Vinegar

**PREPARATION** 15 mins **COOKING** 1 hr 45 mins

900g chicken thigh fillets

¼ cup olive oil

freshly ground black pepper

2 large cloves garlic, chopped

2 teaspoons chopped fresh

rosemary

5 anchovy fillets, chopped

½ cup white wine vinegar

2 tablespoons balsamic

vinegar

20 Kalamata olives, to serve

1 Remove any excess fat from the chicken fillets and cut each into 4 pieces. In a wide heavy-based pan, heat the olive oil and brown the chicken pieces all over, seasoning well with pepper. Transfer to a plate and keep warm.

2 Heat the pan over a low heat and add garlic, rosemary and anchovies. Cook and stir until the mixture is aromatic.

3 Transfer the mixture and the chicken to a slow cooker set on a high heat. Add the white wine vinegar, cover and simmer for about 1½ hours until the chicken is tender.

4 Just before removing from the heat, stir in the balsamic vinegar, which will give the dish a great lift. Serve with silverbeet and potatoes roasted in olive oil with a few sprigs of rosemary and olives.

American Chicken Casserole

serves 4

# American Chicken Casserole

**PREPARATION** 5 mins   **COOKING** 3 hrs 40 mins

2 tablespoons oil

8 chicken drumsticks

salt and freshly ground black pepper

4 onions, sliced

300mL chicken stock

½ teaspoon chilli powder

2 tablespoons plain flour

2 x 400g canned tomatoes

1 x 400g canned red kidney beans, rinsed, drained

50g butter

1   Heat the oil in a large frying pan over medium heat. Add the chicken, season and cook until browned. Add the onions and fry for 1 minute.

2   Heat stock in a small saucepan until simmering.

3   In a preheated slow cooker set on high, sprinkle the chilli powder and flour. Slowly add the stock, stirring constantly. Transfer chicken and onions to slow cooker and add the tomatoes, beans and butter. Cover and cook for 3½ hours on high.

Slow Chicken with Ricotta, Rocket and Red Capsicum

serves 4

# Slow Chicken with Ricotta, Rocket and Red Capsicum

**PREPARATION** 10 mins  **COOKING** 2 hrs

200g fresh ricotta cheese

1 cup chopped rocket

¼ cup toasted pine nuts

100g chargrilled marinated

capsicum, chopped

salt and freshly ground black

pepper

4 chicken breasts, skin on;

each 170g

20g butter

1 cup chicken stock

1  Combine the ricotta, rocket, pine nuts, capsicum and salt and pepper in a small bowl and mix together until smooth.

2  Place 1–2 tablespoons of ricotta mixture under the skin of each chicken breast.

3  Place the chicken breasts in a slow cooker set on high, sprinkle with more salt and pepper, place 1 teaspoon of butter on each breast and pour the stock around the chicken. Cook for 2 hours on high. Serve the chicken with juices and a rocket salad.

Jugged Portuguese Chicken

serves 4

# Jugged Portuguese Chicken

**PREPARATION** 10 mins   **COOKING** 7 hrs 10 mins

60g butter

8 small onions, peeled

1.5 kg whole chicken

3 tomatoes, cut into wedges

100g smoked ham or bacon, diced

2 bay leaves

2 cloves garlic, crushed

2 teaspoons Dijon mustard

¾ cup dry white wine

¼ cup port wine

2 tablespoons brandy

salt and freshly ground black pepper

1  Melt 20g butter in a large heavy-based frying pan over medium heat. Add onions and cook for 2 minutes, stirring constantly. Brush chicken all over with the remaining butter. Add chicken to pan and cook for 4 minutes.

2  In a slow cooker set on low, arrange tomatoes, ham or bacon and bay leaves over base of dish. Add the contents of the frying pan and splash the pan with a little of the white wine and add to the slow cooker as well.

3  Blend together garlic, mustard, remaining white wine, port wine, brandy, salt and pepper. Pour over chicken, cover and cook for 7 hours.

**NOTE** As an alternative you can carefully remove the ceramic insert with the jugged chicken in the last 15 minutes of cooking and put in an oven, preheated to 200°C. Bake with the lid removed to brown the chicken. Cut the chicken into pieces and serve with crispy potatoes and salad.

Duck with Cherries and Radicchio

serves 4

# Duck with Cherries and Radicchio

**PREPARATION** 15 mins   **COOKING** 4 hrs 15 mins

1 duck

1 onion, chopped

300mL chicken stock

450g canned black cherries

finely grated rind of 1 lemon

salt and freshly ground black pepper

1 tablespoon cornflour

1 tablespoon blackcurrant syrup

12 radicchio leaves, washed

## GREMOLATA

rind of 1 lemon, finely diced

2 cloves garlic, finely diced

¼ cup chopped fresh parsley

1  Combine the duck and onion in the slow cooker. Pour over the stock, cherries and half of the cherry juice. Sprinkle with grated lemon rind and seasoning. Cover and cook for 4 hours on high.

2  Remove duck from slow cooker. Cut duck into pieces, then cover and keep warm. Drain cherries from slow cooker and retain 3–4 tablespoons of liquid.

3  Pour remaining cherry juice and retained liquid into a saucepan. Make the cornflour into a paste with the blackcurrant syrup, stir it through the liquid and bring to a boil. Reduce liquid by half and drizzle over the duck.

4  To prepare the gremolata, combine all ingredients in a small bowl.

5  Serve pieces of duck and cherries in radicchio leaves, sprinkled with gremolata.

Chicken Wings Moroccan Style

serves 4

# Chicken Wings Moroccan Style

**PREPARATION** 10 mins   **COOKING** 8 hrs 40 mins

2 tablespoons vegetable oil

1 kg chicken wings

1 large onion, finely chopped

1 clove garlic, crushed

1½ teaspoons grated fresh ginger

½ teaspoon ground turmeric

½ teaspoon ground cumin

1 cinnamon stick

¼ cup cider vinegar

2 cups apricot nectar

salt and freshly ground black pepper

90g dried prunes, pitted

90g dried apricots

1 tablespoon honey

¼ cup lemon juice

fresh parsley sprigs to garnish

1   Heat the oil in a large saucepan. Add the chicken wings, a few at a time, and brown lightly on both sides. Remove to a plate as they brown.

2   Add the onion and cook for 2 minutes. Stir in the garlic and cook for a further minute.

3   Transfer the onion and garlic to a slow cooker on a low setting. Add the chicken, ginger and spices. Stir and turn the wings to coat with spices. Add the vinegar and apricot nectar and season to taste. Cover and cook for 6 hours.

4   Add the prunes, apricots, honey and lemon juice. Cover and simmer for 2 more hours and then remove lid, turn to high and simmer uncovered for 35 minutes. If a thicker sauce is desired, remove the wings and fruit to a serving platter and simmer until the sauce reduces and thickens. Pour the sauce over the wings. Serve immediately on a bed of steamed couscous or rice, garnished with a sprig of parsley.

Chicken Marengo

serves 6

# Chicken Marengo

**PREPARATION** 15 mins   **COOKING** 6 hrs 15 mins

1.75 kg chicken pieces

salt and freshly ground black pepper

2 tablespoons plain flour

1 tablespoon olive oil

20g butter

2 cloves garlic, crushed

1 bouquet garni

¾ cup hot water

2 tablespoons brandy

2 large tomatoes, peeled, chopped

12 button mushrooms, sliced

2 tablespoons chopped fresh parsley to garnish

1  Season the chicken pieces with salt and pepper and sprinkle with half of the flour. Heat oil and butter in a large heavy-based saucepan. Add the chicken and cook over a medium heat until golden, turning frequently.

2  Transfer the chicken to a slow cooker set on low and add garlic, bouquet garni, hot water, brandy, tomatoes and mushrooms. Cover and cook for 6 hours.

3  Approximately 20 minutes before serving combine remaining flour with a little water to make a smooth paste. Stir through chicken to thicken the sauce if necessary. Sprinkle with chopped parsley and serve with steamed rice.

# Hunter's Chicken

**PREPARATION** 15 mins   **COOKING** 3 hrs 15 mins

1.5 kg chicken pieces

salt and freshly ground black pepper

1 cinnamon stick

2 cloves garlic, chopped

1 green capsicum, chopped

2 small onions, sliced

2 sticks celery, chopped

8 small mushrooms, sliced

¼ cup dry sherry

1 cup canned tomatoes, chopped

¼ cup cornflour

¼ cup water

**1** Season chicken pieces with salt and pepper. Place the chicken pieces along with all the other ingredients, except cornflour and water, in a slow cooker. Stir well. Cover and cook on high for 3 hours.

**2** Remove chicken pieces and keep warm. Make a smooth paste of cornflour and water and stir into slow cooker. Return chicken, cover and cook for 15 minutes until the gravy thickens. Serve with steamed couscous.

White meats such as pork are succulent and rich when cooked slowly, either on the bone or seasoned and rolled, as the natural fats render down to add richness to the sauces and the entire dish being cooked develops immense flavour. Marry your pork with flavours such as orange and star anise – flavours that suit both sweet and savoury work especially well when you are cooking in a way that allows the flavour to penetrate all the way through. You will create luscious and memorable dishes worthy of the time spent cooking them.

# Pork

COLLECTORS EDITION

Pork

# Pork

COLLECTORS EDITION

# serves 6 | Gingered Roast Pork

**PREPARATION** 15 mins   **COOKING** 7 hrs

1.5 kg pork loin or leg,
well trimmed, tied with
kitchen string

salt and freshly ground black
pepper

3 Granny Smith apples,
peeled, cored, quartered

1 tablespoon brown sugar

2 teaspoons ground ginger

1 teaspoon salt

1 tablespoon cornflour

1 tablespoon water

1   Rub pork rind with salt and pepper. Arrange apples in base of slow cooker. Place pork on top of apples.

2   Combine brown sugar, ginger and salt. Spoon over top surface of pork. Cover and cook on low for 7 hours.

3   Ten minutes before serving strain off 1 cup of liquid into a small saucepan. Blend cornflour with water to make a smooth paste and stir into liquid. Heat until thickened. Remove string from the pork roll and carve. Serve with sauce, accompanied by the apples and freshly steamed vegetables.

serves 4

# Indonesian Pork Spare Ribs

**PREPARATION** 10 mins   **COOKING** 4 hrs 10 mins

750g pork spare ribs

1½ tablespoons peanut oil

1 teaspoon ground coriander

½ teaspoon ground cumin

½ teaspoon freshly ground

black pepper

2 tablespoons soy sauce

1 tablespoon tamarind

concentrate

1 teaspoon brown sugar

¼ cup water

**PASTE**

2 French shallots, chopped

2 cloves garlic

2 teaspoons finely grated

fresh ginger

¼ cup water

1  Pound the paste ingredients in a mortar and pestle or combine in a small food processor.

2  Chop spare ribs in half. Heat 1 tablespoon of oil in a wok or medium frying pan. Add spare ribs in 2 batches and fry for 2–3 minutes or until ribs are golden and crisp. Remove and set aside.

3  Heat remaining oil and add paste. Cook for 2 minutes, stirring constantly. Add coriander, cumin, black pepper, soy sauce, tamarind and sugar.

4  Turn all ingredients out into slow cooker set on a high heat setting. Return ribs to sauce, add water and cook for 4 hours, basting and turning every hour. Add a little extra water if sauce becomes too thick. Serve with Chinese greens and a side bowl of rice.

Pork Cutlets with Quince

serves 4

# Pork Cutlets with Quince

---

**PREPARATION** 10 mins  **COOKING** 8 hrs 20 mins

---

1 tablespoon olive oil

4 pork cutlets

## SAUCE

½ cup dry white wine

1 clove garlic, crushed

1 medium red onion, sliced

1 medium quince, peeled,
cored, cut into thin wedges

juice of 1 orange

⅓ cup chicken stock

1 cinnamon stick

1 tablespoon honey

1 tablespoon chopped fresh
parsley

salt and freshly ground black
pepper

1  In a slow cooker set on a high heat setting, add white wine, garlic, onion and quince and cook with the lid on for 20 minutes, stirring occasionally.

2  Meanwhile, heat oil in a frying pan. Carefully fry pork cutlets on their sides, browning the pork rind only, for 2–3 minutes. Set meat aside.

3  Stir into slow cooker the orange juice, chicken stock, cinnamon stick and honey. Add the pork and turn down to a low heat setting and cook for 8 hours (or until sauce has thickened slightly). Stir in parsley, salt and pepper, and serve.

Boston Pork and Beans

serves 4

# Boston Pork and Beans

**PREPARATION** 10 mins plus 12 hrs soaking   **COOKING** 4 hrs 10 mins

250g dried haricot beans, soaked overnight, drained

2 tablespoons olive oil

500g bacon or ham hock, diced

1 large onion, chopped

1 clove garlic, crushed

400g canned diced tomatoes

1 bay leaf

2 sprigs fresh thyme

1 sprig fresh marjoram

2 tablespoons dark brown sugar

1 tablespoon golden syrup

1 tablespoon tomato paste

2 teaspoons Angostura bitters

3 teaspoons Dijon mustard

salt and freshly ground black pepper

¼ cup tomato juice

1   Heat the oil in a large frying pan over medium heat. Add meat and cook until browned. Remove meat from pan. Cook onion for 3 minutes. Add garlic and cook for a further 2 minutes.

2   Layer beans, onions and tomatoes in a slow cooker. Top with meat and add the herbs (tied into a bouquet with kitchen string).

3   Mix together sugar, golden syrup, tomato paste, bitters, mustard, salt, pepper and tomato juice. Spoon over ingredients in slow cooker. Cover slow cooker and cook for 4 hours on high.

Chorizo and Lentil Stew

serves 4

# Chorizo and Lentil Stew

**PREPARATION** 20 mins   **COOKING** 4 hrs 40 mins

250g brown lentils, rinsed

4 cups boiling water

4 tomatoes

3½ cups chicken stock

250g chorizo sausage, chopped

1 red onion, sliced

2 garlic cloves, crushed

½ teaspoon dried crushed chillies

salt and freshly ground black pepper

chopped fresh flat-leaf parsley to garnish

1　Place the lentils and boiling water in a slow cooker set on high. Cook for 30 minutes, stirring occasionally. Meanwhile, place the tomatoes in a bowl and cover with boiling water. Leave for 30 seconds, then peel, remove the seeds and chop the flesh. Drain the lentils and return to slow cooker with ¼ cup fresh water and stock.

2　Put the chorizo into a large heavy-based frying pan and cook over a low heat until the fat starts to run out of the sausage. Increase the heat to high and cook, stirring frequently, for 8 minutes or until browned. Add the onions and cook for 2 more minutes.

3　Transfer chorizo and onion to the slow cooker, then stir in the chopped tomatoes, garlic and chillies. Season with salt and pepper and cook, covered, for 4 hours, until quite thick but not too dry. Garnish with parsley.

Swedish Pork Meatballs

serves 6

# Swedish Pork Meatballs

**PREPARATION** 1 hr 45 mins   **COOKING** 5 hrs 20 mins

1½ cups white breadcrumbs

1 cup buttermilk

500g lean pork mince

250g lean beef mince

2 eggs

1 medium onion, finely chopped

2 teaspoons salt

¾ teaspoon dill seeds

¼ teaspoon allspice

⅛ teaspoon ground nutmeg

60g butter

1 cup chicken stock

½ cup dry white wine

freshly ground black pepper

1 cup cream

2 tablespoons fresh parsley leaves to garnish

1  Soak breadcrumbs in buttermilk for 5 minutes. Add meats, eggs, onion, salt, herbs and spices. Mix well, cover and refrigerate for 30 minutes.

2  Shape tablespoon quantities of mixture into balls.

3  Heat butter in a medium frying pan and cook meatballs until lightly browned.

4  Place meatballs into the slow cooker as they are browned. Add stock, wine and pepper. Cover and cook on low for 5 hours.

5  Approximately 20 minutes before serving turn the heat to high and add cream. Serve meatballs garnished with parsley and accompanied by crusty bread.

**NOTE** The meatballs will have a finer texture if the meats are minced together twice (ask your butcher to do this).

Braised Pork with Apples

serves 4

# Braised Pork with Apples

**PREPARATION** 15 mins   **COOKING** 5 hrs 15 mins

1 tablespoon olive oil

4 pork medallions

4 spring onions, thinly sliced

200g button mushrooms, sliced

1 tablespoon plain flour

1 cup vegetable stock

½ cup dry cider

2 teaspoons Dijon or wholegrain mustard

freshly ground black pepper

2 large green apples, peeled, cored, sliced

fresh flat-leaf parsley to garnish

1  Heat half of the oil in a large non-stick frying pan. Add the pork and cook each side for 3 minutes or until browned, then transfer to a slow cooker set on low.

2  Heat the remaining oil in pan and add the spring onions and mushrooms and cook gently for 5 minutes or until softened. Add the flour and cook for 1 minute, stirring. Slowly add the stock and cider, stirring until smooth, then add the mustard and pepper. Bring to the boil and continue stirring for 2–3 minutes, until thickened slightly.

3  Place the apple slices on top of the pork steaks in the slow cooker and pour over the sauce. Cover and cook for 5 hours. Garnish with the parsley.

**NOTE** Pork goes beautifully with the slight tartness of cooked apples. In this succulent slow-cooked casserole, the cider brings out the taste of the apples even more.

Mediterranean Pork Pot Roast

serves 6–8

# Mediterranean Pork Pot Roast

**PREPARATION** 15 mins   **COOKING** 7 hrs 30 mins

2 onions, 1 finely diced and 1 sliced

2 cloves garlic, finely diced

1 large stick celery, finely diced

1 tablespoon finely chopped fresh oregano

1 rasher thick-cut bacon, finely diced

2 tablespoons plain flour

2 kg pork loin roll roast

1  Combine diced onion, garlic, celery, oregano and bacon in a bowl. Lightly flour the pork with 1 tablespoon of flour, then rub with vegetable mixture.

2  Place the remaining sliced onion in a slow cooker. Place the pork on top of the onion. Cover and cook on low for 7½ hours.

3  Ten minutes before serving, remove pork from the cooker and keep warm. Thicken the juices in the cooker with the remaining tablespoon of flour. Slice pork and serve drizzled with juices.

Tuscan Sausage Pot

serves 4

# Tuscan Sausage Pot

**PREPARATION** 15 mins   **COOKING** 3 hrs 40 mins

2 tablespoons olive oil

500g pork sausages

1 red onion, sliced

2 sticks celery, sliced

1 large carrot, diced

1 clove garlic, crushed

4 Roma tomatoes

½ cup dry white wine

salt and freshly ground black

pepper

400g canned cannellini

beans, rinsed

4 cups water

1 teaspoon salt

200g instant polenta

30g butter

chopped fresh flat-leaf

parsley to garnish

1 Heat 1 tablespoon of the oil in a large frying pan and cook the sausages for 5 minutes or until browned, turning occasionally. Remove from the pan. Add the remaining oil and cook the onion, celery, carrot and garlic for 3–4 minutes, until lightly coloured.

2 Meanwhile, put the tomatoes in a bowl and cover with boiling water. Leave for 30 seconds, then peel and cut the flesh into quarters.

3 Place the tomatoes, sausages and sautéed vegetables into a slow cooker set on high and add the wine and the seasoning. Cook for 2 hours.

4 Add the beans and cook for a further 1½ hours.

5 Just before the sausage pot is ready bring water to the boil in a large saucepan and add salt. Sprinkle in the polenta and stir for 5 minutes or until thick and smooth, then add the butter. Serve with the sausage pot, sprinkled with parsley.

**NOTE** This is the Italian version of bangers and mash. Polenta is used instead of potato and the sausages are cooked with lots of vegetables.

Portuguese Pork with Cumin

serves 4

# Portuguese Pork with Cumin

**PREPARATION** 15 mins   **COOKING** 4 hrs 45 mins

3 cloves garlic, crushed

1 teaspoon ground cumin

finely grated rind of 1 lemon

2 tablespoons lemon juice

2 teaspoons Dijon mustard

½ cup dry white wine

¼ cup chopped fresh coriander

750g fillet pork, cut into 2cm pieces

¼ cup olive oil

1 onion, sliced

¾ cup chicken stock

salt and freshly ground black pepper

coriander leaves to garnish

1   Mix together garlic, cumin, lemon rind, lemon juice, mustard, white wine and coriander in a shallow bowl. Add pork and coat well in the mixture.

2   Heat 2 tablespoons of oil in a large frying pan over medium to high heat. Remove pork from marinade with a slotted spoon, reserving marinade. Add pork to frying pan and cook in batches until golden. Remove and set aside. Heat remaining oil and cook onion until soft.

3   Place pork and onion in a slow cooker set on low and add the remaining marinade and chicken stock. Cover and simmer for 4½ hours. Season with salt and pepper and garnish with coriander leaves. Serve pork with lemon wedges and fried potatoes.

# Pork with Tripe Roman Style

serves 4

**PREPARATION** 15 mins   **COOKING** 6 hrs

1  Leaving the tripe in large pieces, place it in a large pan and cover with water. Bring to the boil and drain off the liquid. Add fresh water to just cover, then add the salt, bring to the boil, cover and simmer gently until tender, for about 1 hour. Drain, cool and cut into thin 5cm strips.

2  Meanwhile, to make the sauce, in a slow cooker on a high heat add the olive oil. Add the tomatoes, onion, garlic and the basil. Cook for 45 minutes, stirring once, until the sauce thickens. Remove the basil or oregano and season well with salt and pepper.

3  Add the tripe and pork pieces to the slow cooker, stirring to mix thoroughly. Cook on a low heat for about 5 hours. Add salt and pepper if necessary and serve in a bowl with Parmesan scattered over.

600g honeycomb tripe

1 teaspoon salt

1 quantity tomato sauce (see below)

300g pork neck pieces

freshly ground black pepper

grated Parmesan cheese

## TOMATO SAUCE

½ cup olive oil

2 large onions, finely sliced

2 large cloves garlic, chopped

900g ripe red tomatoes, peeled, seeded, roughly chopped

10 basil leaves

salt and freshly ground black pepper

The perfumed flavour of lamb combines perfectly with slow cooking casseroles and rich hearty stews to create mouthwatering treats that work with pastas and grains and good old-fashioned mashed potato. Let your slow cooker do the work of breaking down and thickening all your lamb and vegetable combinations, leaving you plenty of time in the final hour to prepare your grains or root-vegetable mash as the perfect accompaniment. Rosemary and citrus zests work beautifully in a slow cooker with lamb, and as always with rich old-fashioned foods, don't forget the garlic.

# Lamb

COLLECTORS EDITION

Lamb

# Lamb

COLLECTORS EDITION

# Greek Meatballs with Egg-Lemon Sauce

serves 4

**PREPARATION** 15 mins   **COOKING** 6 hrs 10 mins

1½ cups beef stock

500g lean lamb mince

1 small onion, chopped

5 egg yolks

1 teaspoon chopped
fresh mint

1 teaspoon chopped
fresh oregano

1 tablespoon chopped
fresh parsley

salt and freshly ground black
pepper

2 tablespoons rice

juice of 1 lemon

1　Place 1 cup of stock in a slow cooker on high. Cover and heat.

2　Combine lamb, onion, 1 egg yolk, mint, oregano and parsley in a large bowl. Season with salt and pepper and add remaining stock. Roll tablespoon quantities into balls, then roll lightly in rice.

3　Transfer meatballs into slow cooker. Cover, turn to low and cook for 6 hours.

4　In a medium-sized bowl beat remaining egg yolks, slowly adding lemon juice until combined. Slowly add most of the hot stock from slow cooker, beating constantly until well combined and mixture thickens. Stir over low heat in a small saucepan if necessary. Serve the sauce drizzled over the meatballs.

Irish Stew

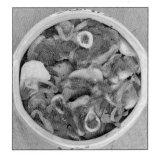

serves 4

# Irish Stew

**PREPARATION** 10 mins   **COOKING** 5 hrs 30 mins

2 large onions, sliced

1 kg lamb neck pieces

2 teaspoons mixed dried herbs

salt and freshly ground black

pepper

2–3 large potatoes, peeled,

sliced

2 cups chicken stock

1 tablespoon chopped fresh

parsley to garnish

1  Place one quarter of the onions in a slow cooker and place the lamb on top. Sprinkle with herbs and season well.

2  Combine remaining onions and potatoes and place over lamb. Season well, pour over stock and cook for 5½ hours on high. Serve sprinkled with freshly chopped parsley and steamed vegetables.

Lamb Shanks with Broad Beans, Olives and Risoni

serves 4–6

# Lamb Shanks with Broad Beans, Olives and Risoni

**PREPARATION** 20 mins   **COOKING** 9 hrs 20 mins

2 tablespoons olive oil

2 cloves garlic, crushed

4 lamb shanks

1 onion, chopped

2 cups beef stock

4 sprigs fresh oregano

2 tablespoons tomato paste

2 cups water

1 cup risoni

1 cup broad beans

½ cup black olives

2 teaspoons chopped fresh oregano

salt and freshly ground black pepper

1　Heat the oil in a large saucepan, add the garlic, lamb shanks and onion and cook for 5 minutes or until the shanks are lightly browned.

2　Transfer to a slow cooker set on low. Add the beef stock, oregano sprigs, tomato paste and water. Cook for 8 hours.

3　Remove the shanks, slice the meat off the bone and set aside.

4　Turn slow cooker onto high and add the risoni and cook for a further 45 minutes. Add the beans, olives, meat, oregano, salt and pepper, cook for 30 minutes more and serve.

**NOTE** If broad beans are large, peel off outer skin.

African Bobotie Curry

serves 4

# African Bobotie Curry

**PREPARATION** 10 mins   **COOKING** 3 hrs 15 mins

1 tablespoon vegetable oil

1 onion, finely chopped

2 thick slices of white bread, broken into pieces (crusts removed)

1⅕ cups milk

500g lean lamb mince

2 tablespoons curry paste

2 cloves garlic, crushed

salt and freshly ground black pepper

juice of ½ lemon

50g dried apricots, chopped

50g raisins

60g flaked almonds

2 eggs

1   Heat the oil in a large heavy-based frying pan, add the onion and fry for 5 minutes to soften. Place the bread in a bowl with the milk and leave to soak.

2   Meanwhile, add the lamb to the pan and cook for 10 minutes or until browned, breaking it up with a wooden spoon. Transfer the lamb to a slow cooker set on high and add the curry paste, garlic and seasoning and cook for 30 minutes. Add the lemon juice, apricots and raisins and 30g of the almonds and mix well.

3   Lift the bread out of the milk and squeeze gently to remove some of the liquid. Reserve the milk and add the bread to the slow cooker. Cover and cook for 2 hours.

4   Preheat the oven to 180°C. Whisk the eggs into the remaining milk and season. Pour over the lamb mixture and sprinkle with the remaining almonds. Transfer the ovenproof part of the slow cooker to the oven and cook for 30 minutes or until the top has set and is golden.

**NOTE** This is South Africa's answer to shepherd's pie. Sweet and spicy minced lamb is hidden under a golden topping, scattered with flaked almonds. Serve hot with a green salad.

Lamb and Spinach Curry

serves 4

# Lamb and Spinach Curry

**PREPARATION** 15 mins   **COOKING** 7 hrs 25 mins

2 tablespoons vegetable oil

2 onions, chopped

2 cloves garlic, chopped

2cm piece fresh root ginger, finely chopped

1 cinnamon stick

¼ teaspoon ground cloves

3 cardamom pods

750g diced lamb

1 tablespoon ground cumin

1 tablespoon ground coriander

⅓ cup natural yoghurt

2 tablespoons tomato paste

¾ cup beef stock

salt and freshly ground black pepper

100g baby spinach, chopped

2 tablespoons flaked almonds, toasted

1  Heat the oil in a large heavy-based saucepan. Add onions, garlic, ginger, cinnamon, cloves and cardamom and cook for 5 minutes.

2  Add the lamb and cook for 5 minutes, turning, until it begins to brown.

3  Transfer to a slow cooker set on high. Mix in the cumin and coriander, then add the yoghurt 1 tablespoon at a time, stirring well each time.

4  Mix together the tomato paste and the stock and add to the lamb. Season to taste. Reduce the heat to low, cover and cook for 7 hours.

5  Stir in the spinach, cover and simmer for another 15 minutes or until the mixture has reduced slightly. Remove the cinnamon stick and the cardamom pods and mix in the almonds. Serve with rice.

**NOTE** There's plenty of flavour but no chilli in this dish, so it'll be a hit even with those who don't like hot curries. You can serve it with pilau or plain rice.

Minced Lamb and Eggplant Casserole

serves 4

# Minced Lamb and Eggplant Casserole

**PREPARATION** 10 mins   **COOKING** 2 hrs 15 mins

1 tablespoon olive oil

1 small eggplant, sliced

250g lean lamb mince

3 large ripe tomatoes,

peeled, sliced

salt and freshly ground black

pepper

6 fresh basil leaves, finely

shredded

125g Swiss cheese, grated

1   Heat oil in a large frying pan over medium heat. Add eggplant and cook until golden brown. Drain on sheets of absorbent paper.

2   Add lamb and cook for 3–4 minutes or until browned. Drain off any excess fat.

3   In a small casserole dish that fits into your slow cooker, arrange a layer of eggplant slices, a layer of minced lamb and a layer of sliced tomato, sprinkled with salt and pepper and half of the basil. Cover with grated cheese. Repeat layers until casserole dish is filled, ending with a cheese layer.

4   Place casserole in a slow cooker and cook on high for approximately 2 hours. If preferred, casserole may be placed under griller for a minute or two to brown cheese topping. Serve with a large leafy green salad.

Slow-Simmered Lamb Shanks with Couscous

serves 4

# Slow-Simmered Lamb Shanks with Couscous

**PREPARATION** 15 mins   **COOKING** 5 hrs 10 mins

4 lamb shanks, French cut

2 cups canned chopped tomatoes

1 cup dry red wine

1 bay leaf

6 sprigs fresh thyme

1 cinnamon stick

200g butternut pumpkin, chopped

2 zucchini, chopped

8 dried apricots

8 dried prunes

1 cup couscous

2 cups boiling water

2 tablespoons flaked almonds, toasted

1　Heat a large frying pan over a high heat and add lamb and cook until browned. Transfer to a slow cooker set on high.

2　Add the tomatoes, wine, bay leaf, thyme and cinnamon stick. Cover and cook for 3 hours.

3　Add the pumpkin, zucchini, apricots and prunes and cook for a further 2 hours on a low setting or until the vegetables are soft and the lamb starts to come away from the bone.

4　Meanwhile, put the couscous in a large bowl, cover with boiling water and allow to stand for 10 minutes or until all the liquid is absorbed.

5　Serve the lamb shanks on top of the couscous, garnished with the flaked almonds.

**NOTE** The term Frenched refers to the cutting and scraping of all meat, fat and gristle from the bone, leaving the meaty part virtually fat-free.

Lamb Casserole with Couscous and Gremolata

serves 4

# Lamb Casserole with Couscous and Gremolata

**PREPARATION** 30 mins  **COOKING** 10 hrs 15 mins

2 tablespoons plain flour

salt and freshly ground black pepper

750g diced lamb, trimmed of excess fat

2–3 tablespoons extra virgin olive oil

1 yellow capsicum, chopped

1 green capsicum, chopped

2 cups canned chopped tomatoes

### GREMOLATA

1 clove garlic, finely chopped

3 tablespoons finely chopped fresh parsley

grated rind of 1 lemon

### COUSCOUS

2 cups couscous

1 tablespoon extra virgin olive oil

1 large onion, sliced

1 Season the flour with salt and pepper and spread it on a large plate. Toss the lamb in the seasoned flour until coated. Heat the oil in a large frying pan, add lamb and cook over medium heat for 2–3 minutes each side, until browned. Transfer the browned meat to a slow cooker set on low, using a slotted spoon.

2 Add the capsicums and the tomatoes to the slow cooker and cook for 10 hours. Meanwhile, mix all the gremolata ingredients together.

3 Prepare the couscous according to the packet instructions, then fluff it up with a fork. Heat the oil in a small frying pan and cook the onion over a medium heat for 10 minutes until golden brown. Add to the couscous and mix well. Sprinkle the gremolata over the lamb casserole and serve with the couscous.

**NOTE** Gremolata is a mixture of finely cut parsley, garlic and lemon zest. Adding this to the casserole just before serving adds a fresh new dimension of flavour.

Indian Meatballs in Tomato Sauce

serves 4

# Indian Meatballs in Tomato Sauce

**PREPARATION** 20 mins   **COOKING** 5 hrs 20 mins

500g lean lamb mince

½ cup natural yoghurt

5cm piece fresh ginger, grated

1 green chilli, deseeded, finely chopped

¼ cup chopped fresh coriander

2 teaspoons ground cumin

2 teaspoons ground coriander

salt and freshly ground black pepper

2 tablespoons olive oil

1 onion, chopped

2 cloves garlic, chopped

½ teaspoon ground turmeric

1 teaspoon garam masala

170mL water

400g canned chopped tomatoes

1   Combine the lamb, 1 tablespoon of yoghurt, ginger, chilli, 2 tablespoons of chopped coriander, cumin and ground coriander in a large bowl and season with salt and pepper. Shape the mixture into 16 balls.

2   Heat 1 tablespoon of oil in a large saucepan, add meatballs and cook for 10 minutes, turning until browned (you may have to cook them in batches). Drain on absorbent paper and set aside.

3   In a slow cooker on a high setting add the remaining olive oil, onion and garlic and stir. Mix the turmeric and garam masala with 1 tablespoon of the water, then add to onion and garlic. Add remaining yoghurt, 1 tablespoon at a time, stirring well each time.

4   Add the tomatoes, meatballs and remaining water to the mixture and bring to temperature. Cook for 5 hours, stirring occasionally. Sprinkle over the rest of the coriander to garnish and serve on a bed of rice.

Tarragon Lamb

serves 4

# Tarragon Lamb

**PREPARATION** 10 mins   **COOKING** 10 hrs 20 mins

60g butter

1 kg log of lamb

450mL chicken stock

⅔ cup dry white wine

1 bunch fresh tarragon

salt and freshly ground black pepper

1½ tablespoons cornflour

1 tablespoon water

2 tablespoons pouring cream

1 Melt 40g of the butter in a large heavy-based frying pan over medium heat. Add the lamb and cook for 3 minutes or until browned.

2 Transfer to a slow cooker on a low setting and add the remaining butter, stock and wine. Cover and cook for 10 hours.

3 Remove the meat and keep warm. Add the tarragon and seasoning to the cooker, turn to high and reduce the liquid by half. Thicken with the cornflour mixed with the water to form a paste, then add the cream.

4 Taste and adjust the seasoning, then remove the tarragon. Slice the lamb and serve with the reduced sauce and roasted vegetables.

# Lamb Shanks with Root Vegetables

serves 4

**PREPARATION** 20 mins   **COOKING** 8 hrs 40 mins

2 tablespoons olive oil

2 parsnips, cut into large chunks

1 medium sweet potato,
cut into large chunks

6 pickling onions

2 cloves garlic, crushed

4 lamb shanks

¾ cup beef stock

¼ cup water

½ cup dry red wine

1 tablespoon tomato paste

1 sprig rosemary

1 bouquet garni

salt and freshly ground black
pepper

1   Heat 1 tablespoon of the oil in a large heavy-based saucepan, add the root vegetables and cook until brown. Set aside on a plate. Add the extra oil to the pan and brown the garlic and lamb for a few minutes.

2   Transfer the lamb and garlic to a slow cooker set on high and add the stock, water, red wine, tomato paste, rosemary, bouquet garni, pepper and salt. Cook for 30 minutes, then reduce the heat to low and cook for a further 7 hours.

3   Add the vegetables to the slow cooker and continue to cook for another hour, until everything is cooked. Before serving, remove the bouquet garni and check the seasoning.

Beef is the ultimate meat to stand up against flavours such as bay leaf, garlic, peppercorn and red wine. Use it to create rich, hearty meals that are deep in traditional flavour and a real family pleaser in every mouthful. Slow-cooked beef is perfect for that winter meal when everyone is feeling the chill and looking for comfort, marrying perfectly with a glass of full-bodied red wine. It's also good in small portions in the warmer months – think of serving a beef ragu on bruschetta or accompanied by a salad of equally robust flavours such as fresh tomato and witlof and pecorino cheese. Delicious whatever the season.

# Beef

COLLECTORS EDITION

# Beef

COLLECTORS EDITION

| # Beef Carbonade

**PREPARATION** 15 mins   **COOKING** 10 hrs 25 mins

2 tablespoons vegetable oil

1 kg gravy beef, cut into 2cm cubes

1 large onion, thinly sliced

1 tablespoon plain flour

2 tablespoons brown sugar

1½ cups stout

2 cups beef stock

1 tablespoon tomato paste

1 bouquet garni

salt and freshly ground black pepper

chopped fresh parsley to garnish

1   Heat the oil in a large frying pan over medium heat. Add one-third of the beef and cook until browned. Remove from the pan while you cook the remaining batches, adding more oil if necessary. Set the beef aside.

2   Lower the heat, add the onion and cook for 5 minutes, stirring. Sprinkle in the flour and sugar and stir for 1–2 minutes, then add ½ cup of the stout and swirl to collect all of the flavour from the pan. Pour into a slow cooker set on low. Add the remaining stout, stock, sautéed beef, tomato paste and bouquet garni. Season and stir well, then cover.

3   Cook for 10 hours. Stir 2–3 times during cooking, adding a little water if necessary. Discard the bouquet garni and season again if necessary.

serves 4

# Osso Bucco

**PREPARATION** 20 mins   **COOKING** 6 hrs 45 mins

2 tablespoons olive oil

1 kg veal osso buco

1–2 tablespoons plain flour

1 clove garlic, crushed

1 onion, finely chopped

1 carrot, finely diced

2 sticks celery, finely diced

½ cup dry white wine

4 Roma tomatoes, peeled, chopped

⅔ cup beef stock

2 tablespoons tomato paste

1 tablespoon chopped fresh basil

1 tablespoon chopped fresh parsley

salt and freshly ground black pepper

1   Heat oil in a large frying pan.

2   Coat osso buco with flour and cook in pan for 3 minutes each side. Remove from the pan and set aside.

3   Add the garlic, onion, carrot and celery to the pan and cook for 5 minutes. Add wine and cook until evaporated.

4   Add the tomatoes, stock and tomato paste to a slow cooker set on low. Add the veal, vegetables and herbs, then season. Cover and simmer for 6½ hours until the meat starts to come away from the bone. Serve with crusty bread.

Mexican-Style Beef

serves 4

# Mexican-Style Beef

**PREPARATION** 20 mins   **COOKING** 9 hrs 10 mins

4 thin-cut beef sirloin steaks

4 strips rindless bacon, finely chopped

1 tablespoon chopped fresh parsley

½ teaspoon dried marjoram

1 cup fresh breadcrumbs

½ cup plain flour

salt and freshly ground black pepper

toothpicks

1 tablespoon olive oil

1 teaspoon chilli powder

1 onion, diced

2 cloves garlic, crushed

1 red capsicum, diced

1 cup beef stock

2 cups canned red kidney beans, rinsed, drained

1  Place the beef between sheets of non-stick baking paper and flatten. Heat a large frying pan over medium heat. Add bacon and cook for 3 minutes, draining off any excess fat. Remove from the heat and mix with the parsley, marjoram and breadcrumbs.

2  Combine the flour, salt and pepper in a shallow dish. Divide the bacon mixture between slices of the beef, then roll up each slice from the short end, turn it in the seasoned flour and secure it with a tooth pick.

3  Heat the oil in a large frying pan over medium heat, add the beef and cook for 2 minutes, turning, until browned. Remove from pan and place in a slow cooker set on low. Add the chilli powder, onion, garlic and capsicum. Gently pour over the stock. Cover the dish then cook for 6 hours. Add the kidney beans and cook for another 3 hours. Remove the cocktail sticks to serve.

Drunken Beef

serves 4

# Drunken Beef

**PREPARATION** 5 mins   **COOKING** 9 hrs 10 mins

2 onions, diced

2 carrots, sliced

6 button mushrooms, sliced

⅔ cup beer

¼ cup olive oil

450g gravy beef, diced

2 tablespoons tomato paste

salt and freshly ground black pepper

1 teaspoon fresh thyme

1 bay leaf

1 tablespoon plain flour

1   In a slow cooker set on high, cook the vegetables in the beer and 2 tablespoons of oil for 10 minutes. Add the meat on top of the vegetables and spoon over the tomato paste. Add the seasoning and herbs. Cook for 1 hour on high then reduce the heat to a low setting.

2   Add the remaining oil and the flour. Stir to combine all ingredients and cook on a low setting for 8 hours.

3   Remove the bay leaf, taste and adjust the seasoning. Serve with toast, if desired.

Mediterranean Beef and Olive Casserole

serves 6

# Mediterranean Beef and Olive Casserole

**PREPARATION** 30 mins plus 2 hrs marinating   **COOKING** 6 hrs 12 mins

1.3 kg lean gravy beef, cut into 5cm pieces

2 tablespoons olive oil

24 pitted black olives, plus 12 to garnish

4 tomatoes, quartered, deseeded

salt and freshly ground black pepper

chopped fresh parsley to garnish

grated rind of 1 lemon to garnish

## MARINADE

juice of ½ lemon

2 medium onions, chopped

2 cloves garlic, crushed

3 bay leaves

3 sprigs fresh thyme

½ teaspoon fresh oregano

2 tablespoons chopped fresh parsley

1 small bulb fennel, chopped

2 carrots, sliced

8 whole black peppercorns

2 tablespoons olive oil

3 cups dry white wine

1  Combine marinade ingredients, then add the meat and coat. Cover and refrigerate for 2 hours.

2  Remove the meat, reserving the marinade. Heat 1 tablespoon of the oil in a large frying pan over medium heat. Add half the meat and cook for 6 minutes, turning once. Put prepared meat into a slow cooker set on high, then fry the remaining meat and add to slow cooker as well. Stir in the marinade and 24 olives. Cover and cook for 1 hour.

3  Press the meat down with the back of a wooden spoon and top with the tomatoes. Season lightly and drizzle over the remaining oil. Cover the dish again and cook for 5 hours.

4  Adjust seasoning, then sprinkle over the parsley, lemon rind and remaining olives to serve.

Beef Braised in Red Wine

serves 4

# Beef Braised in Red Wine

**PREPARATION** 20 mins   **COOKING** 4 hrs 10 mins

¼ cup olive oil

700g gravy beef, trimmed of fat, cut into 6cm chunks

6 French shallots, finely chopped

2 cloves garlic, crushed

2 sticks celery, sliced

200g button mushrooms, sliced

½ teaspoon ground allspice

1½ cups full-bodied red wine

1 cup tomato purée

2 sprigs fresh thyme

salt and freshly ground black pepper

1  Heat the oil in a large saucepan and cook the meat over high heat, stirring, for 5 minutes until browned. Remove from pan, then add the shallots, garlic and celery. Cook, stirring, for 4 minutes until browned. Add the mushrooms and cook for 1 minute or until softened.

2  In a slow cooker set on high add the allspice, wine and tomato purée, then all of the fried ingredients. Add 1 sprig of thyme and the seasoning. Cover and cook for 4 hours.

3  Season again if necessary, then serve garnished with the remaining thyme and mashed potato.

Farmers Casserole

# Farmers Casserole

**PREPARATION** 25 mins **COOKING** 4 hrs

450g gravy beef, trimmed of fat, cut into 25mm cubes

2 carrots, diced

2 leeks, sliced

1 onion, diced

1 cup beef stock

salt and freshly ground black pepper

400g canned butter beans, rinsed, drained

50g frozen peas

## CHEESE DUMPLINGS

100g self-raising flour

1 teaspoon finely chopped fresh parsley

50g Cheddar cheese, grated

50g butter, cut into small cubes

2 tablespoons water

1 Place the meal and the vegetables in a slow cooker set on a high setting. Stir in the stock and season well. Cover and cook for 3½ hours.

2 Meanwhile, make the dumplings by combining all the dry ingredients in a bowl. Using your fingertips, rub in the butter and water to form a soft dough.

3 Preheat the oven to 180°C.

4 Shape the dough into 12 equal dumplings. Stir the butter beans and peas into the casserole, taste and adjust the seasoning.

5 Arrange the dumplings over the top and put the uncovered dish in the oven for 30 minutes or until the dumplings are golden.

**NOTE** This recipe requires you to finish the dumplings in the oven so you will need to use a slow cooker with a cooking dish that can be removed from the electrical component and safely put into the oven.

serves 4

# Oxtail with
# Black Olives

PREPARATION 10 mins   COOKING 9 hrs 45 mins

2 small or 1 large oxtail,
trimmed of fat

¼ cup dry white wine

⅓ cup brandy

1½ cups hot beef stock

3 sprigs fresh rosemary

grated rind of 1 orange

2 cloves garlic, crushed

salt and freshly ground black
pepper

1 cup pitted black olives

1  Heat a medium non-stick frying pan over high heat. Add oxtail and cook for 2 minutes or until browned.

2  Place oxtail in a slow cooker, add wine and brandy, then cover and cook on high for 30 minutes to bring oxtail to temperature.

3  Add stock, rosemary, orange rind and garlic. Season with salt and freshly ground pepper. Cover and cook for 8 hours on low.

4  Add the olives and cook for a further hour. You may want to reduce the sauce further by straining it into a small saucepan and rapidly boiling it for 5 minutes or until sauce has thickened. Serve on a bed of steamed rice.

NOTE Ask your butcher to cut the oxtail into joints.

Beef with Artichokes, Olives and Oregano

serves 4

# Beef with Artichokes, Olives and Oregano

**PREPARATION** 20 mins   **COOKING** 8 hrs 10 mins

2 tablespoons olive oil

750g Scotch fillet

1 clove garlic, crushed

1 bunch spring onions, trimmed, halved

½ cup dry white wine

1 cup beef stock

1 tablespoon tomato paste

2 teaspoons chopped fresh oregano

salt and freshly ground black pepper

2 globe artichokes, trimmed and cut into quarters*

⅓ cup black olives

1  In a large heavy-based frying pan heat 1 tablespoon of olive oil, add meat and sear quickly on all sides. Take out and set aside.

2  Heat extra olive oil, add garlic and spring onions, and cook for 3 minutes. Take off the heat then add a splash of white wine to collect all of the flavours from the pan.

3  Pour into a slow cooker set on low, add the remaining white wine, then add beef stock, tomato paste, oregano and salt and pepper. Stir to combine, return meat to dish, add artichokes, cover and cook for 8 hours.

4  Add olives in the last 20 minutes of cooking time.

5  Slice the meat and arrange with vegetables; pour the sauce over meat and vegetables to serve.

*Trim artichokes of outer leaves and stems. Place in a bowl of water with lemon juice. This stops the artichokes from going brown.

Mediterranean Beef Stew with Chickpeas

serves 6

# Mediterranean Beef Stew with Chickpeas

**PREPARATION** 15 mins  **COOKING** 8 hrs 10 mins

2 tablespoons oil

1 kg lean stewing beef, trimmed, cut into large cubes

2 onions, sliced

2 cloves garlic, chopped

1 eggplant, diced

1 cup beef stock

400g canned whole peeled tomatoes, chopped

¼ cup tapioca

1 teaspoon ground cinnamon

1 bay leaf

2 teaspoons salt

freshly ground black pepper

400g canned chickpeas, rinsed, drained

fresh oregano leaves to garnish

1  Heat the oil in a large frying pan over a medium heat. Add meat and cook for 5 minutes, turning occasionally. Add the onions and garlic and cook for a further 5 minutes, stirring constantly. Drain off any excess fats. Place the beef mixture and eggplant in a slow cooker.

2  Combine stock with juice from canned tomatoes, tapioca, cinnamon, bay leaf, salt and pepper and pour into slow cooker; stir well. Cover and cook on low setting for 8 hours.

3  Approximately 30 minutes before serving turn to high, stir in chickpeas and tomatoes and cook for the remaining time. Serve garnished with fresh oregano leaves.

| French Onion Stew

**PREPARATION** 20 mins   **COOKING** 7 hrs

1.5 kg lean stewing beef, trimmed, cut into large cubes

2 tablespoons tapioca

1¾ cup beef stock

100g mushrooms, sliced

60g butter

6 medium onions, thinly sliced

pinch salt

¼ cup double cream

fresh thyme leaves to garnish

1  Combine beef, tapioca, stock and mushrooms in a slow cooker, cover and cook on high for 4 hours.

2  Meanwhile, melt butter in a large heavy-based frying pan over low heat. Add onion and cook, stirring, for 45 minutes or until caramelised and dark brown in colour. Add the caramelised onions to the slow cooker and stir to combine. Continue to cook all ingredients together for remaining time.

3  Just before serving stir through cream. Serve the stew on a bed of rice, garnished with fresh thyme.

Slow cooking vegetables is a fast way to bring all of the flavours out and create hearty and healthy food at the same time. Cooking with this technique allows legumes and pulses to blend perfectly with an array of vegetables, as slow cooking develops the flavour and melts all of the different characteristics together into a complex dish. It's an ideal way to take care of either those vegetables that have been sitting in the refrigerator becoming a little neglected or those that have been freshly picked from the garden. Gentle-flavoured herbs such as tarragon and chervil tossed through at the end of the cooking process add a degree of distinction.

# Vegetables

COLLECTORS EDITION

# Vegetables

Vegetables

COLLECTORS EDITION

serves 4 | # Root Vegetable Curry

**PREPARATION** 20 mins   **COOKING** 3 hrs 20 mins

freshly ground black pepper

chopped fresh coriander

to garnish

1  Heat the oil in a large saucepan. Add the onion, chilli, garlic and ginger and cook, stirring occasionally, for 3 minutes. Stir in the flour, coriander, cumin and turmeric and cook gently, stirring, for 2 minutes to release the flavours.

2  Transfer to a slow cooker set on a high heat setting and stir in the stock, then add the tomato purée, diced root vegetables and carrots. Season with pepper and mix well.

3  Cover and cook for 3¼ hours or until the vegetables are tender. Garnish with coriander.

**NOTE** This spicy curry is based on a traditional Moroccan dish; try serving it with hot fluffy couscous.

1 tablespoon olive oil

1 onion, chopped

1 green chilli, deseeded, chopped

1 clove garlic, finely chopped

2 teaspoons grated fresh ginger

2 tablespoons plain flour

2 teaspoons ground coriander

2 teaspoons ground cumin

2 teaspoons ground turmeric

300mL vegetable stock

200mL tomato purée

750g mixed root vegetables, such as potato, sweet potato, celeriac and swede, diced

2 carrots, thinly sliced

Argentinean Bean and Vegetable Stew

serves 4

# Argentinean Bean and Vegetable Stew

**PREPARATION** 25 mins   **COOKING** 2 hrs 15 mins

1 tablespoon olive oil

1 onion, finely diced

2 cloves garlic, crushed

1 red capsicum, diced

1 jalapeño chilli, deseeded and diced

1 teaspoon sweet paprika

400g canned diced tomatoes

2 cups vegetable stock

250g baby potatoes, cut into quarters

300g sweet potato, diced

1 carrot, sliced

1 cup fresh peas

400g canned cannellini beans, rinsed, drained

3 cups shredded savoy cabbage

2 tablespoons freshly chopped coriander

salt and freshly ground black pepper

1   Heat oil in a large frying pan over medium heat. Cook onion, garlic, capsicum and chilli until soft. Add sweet paprika and cook until aromatic.

2   Transfer contents of the frying pan into a slow cooker set on high and add tomatoes and vegetable stock. Stir to combine, then add potato, sweet potato and carrot. Bring to the boil. Reduce heat to low. Cover and simmer for 1½ hours until vegetables are tender.

3   Add peas, beans, cabbage and coriander and season with salt and pepper. Simmer for a further 30 minutes or until cabbage is cooked.

4   Serve with crusty bread.

serves 4

# Mushroom and Barley 'Risotto'

**PREPARATION** 15 mins   **COOKING** 4 hrs 20 mins

1 tablespoon olive oil

1 onion, diced

250g button mushrooms, coarsely chopped

3 large Portobello mushrooms, sliced

¼ cup chopped fresh parsley

1 tablespoon chopped fresh thyme

2 cloves garlic, crushed

¾ cup pearl barley

4 cups vegetable stock

2 tablespoons tomato paste

salt and freshly ground black pepper

¼ cup grated Parmesan cheese

1  Heat oil in a large heavy-based saucepan over medium heat. Add onion and sauté for 4 minutes. Add all mushrooms and sauté until golden brown, about 15 minutes. Add the parsley, thyme, garlic and barley and stir for 1 minute.

2  Transfer to a slow cooker set on high, add 4 cups of stock, cover and cook until liquid is almost absorbed and barley is almost tender, about 3 hours.

3  Stir in tomato paste, check for seasoning and cook for a further hour. Until barley is tender and mixture is creamy.

4  Stir in cheese and season again if necessary.

Rich Bean and Vegetable Stew

serves 4

# Rich Bean and Vegetable Stew

**PREPARATION** 20 mins plus 20 mins soaking   **COOKING** 1 hr 35 mins

125g dried porcini mushrooms

¼ cup olive oil

250g field mushrooms, chopped

2 carrots, finely diced

1 large potato, diced

250g fine green beans, chopped

2 teaspoons dried thyme

2 teaspoons dried sage

2 cloves garlic, crushed

300mL dry red wine

2¼ cups vegetable stock

salt and freshly ground black pepper

250g frozen broad beans

310g canned cannellini beans, rinsed, drained

250g canned flageolet beans, rinsed, drained

1  Cover the porcini mushrooms with 600mL of boiling water, then soak for 20 minutes. Meanwhile, heat the oil in a large saucepan, then add the fresh mushrooms, carrots, potato and green beans and fry gently for 3 minutes.

2  Transfer to a slow cooker set on a high heat setting and add the thyme, sage and garlic, the porcini with their soaking liquid, and the red wine, stock and seasoning. Cook for 45 minutes.

3  Stir in the broad beans, cover and cook for a further 30 minutes. Add the cannellini and flageolet beans to the mixture, then simmer for 15 minutes to heat through.

**NOTE** This satisfying winter dish is perfect eaten with a hunk of crusty bread to mop up the rich red wine sauce.

Kidney Beans in Plum Sauce

serves 4

# Kidney Beans in Plum Sauce

**PREPARATION** 5 mins    **COOKING** 3 hrs 30 mins

200g dried red kidney beans

2½ cups water

1 tablespoon chopped
fresh basil

1 tablespoon chopped
fresh coriander, plus extra
leaves to garnish

1 tablespoon chopped
fresh parsley

¼ teaspoon cayenne pepper

salt to taste

1 small clove garlic

⅓ cup plum jam

2 teaspoons red wine vinegar

1　Rinse kidney beans well in a strainor under running water. Add the beans and water to a slow cooker set on high. Cook for 2½ hours.

2　Meanwhile, place the basil, coriander, parsley, cayenne pepper, salt and garlic in a food processor and blend to a paste. Add the jam and vinegar and pulse to combine.

3　After 2½ hours add the paste to the beans and stir gently to coat the beans with the dressing. Turn slow cooker onto low and cook for 1 more hour to allow flavours to penetrate. Garnish with coriander leaves. Can be served warm or at room temperature.

Okra and Bean Stew

serves 4

# Okra and Bean Stew

**PREPARATION** 10 mins  **COOKING** 3 hrs

2 x 440g canned tomatoes

250g small okra

2 eggplants, chopped

2 onions, chopped

2 cloves garlic, crushed

1 fresh red chilli, deseeded

and chopped

2 teaspoons olive oil

440g canned red kidney

beans, rinsed, drained

½ cup dry red wine

1 teaspoon brown sugar

¼ cup chopped fresh basil

salt and freshly ground black

pepper

1 Add tomatoes, okra, eggplant, onion, garlic, chilli and olive oil to a slow cooker set on high and cook for 30 minutes.

2 Add beans, wine and sugar and cook for a further 2½ hours.

3 Just before serving stir in basil, salt and pepper to taste.

Spiced Tomato, Pumpkin and Chickpea Tagine

serves 6

# Spiced Tomato, Pumpkin and Chickpea Tagine

**PREPARATION** 10 mins   **COOKING** 2 hrs 25 mins

1 tablespoon olive oil

1 onion, chopped

1 teaspoon ground coriander

1 teaspoon ground cumin

1 teaspoon allspice

1 green chilli, sliced

400g canned chopped tomatoes

2 x 400g canned chickpeas, rinsed, drained

400g pumpkin, diced

2 cups reduced-salt vegetable stock

⅓ cup couscous

½ cup natural yoghurt

1 tablespoon chopped fresh parsley to garnish

1 tablespoon chopped fresh mint to garnish

1  Heat the oil in a large frying pan. Add the onion and cook over a medium heat for 5 minutes or until the onion softens. Add the spices and chilli and cook for 2 minutes or until fragrant.

2  Transfer to a slow cooker set on high, then stir in the tomatoes, chickpeas, pumpkin and stock and cook for 2 hours.

3  Add the couscous, stir and cover, then turn the cooker off. Let sit for 15 minutes until the couscous is soft.

4  Serve topped with a dollop of yoghurt. Sprinkle with parsley and mint.

serves 6

# Mexican Chilli Beans

**PREPARATION** 10 mins   **COOKING** 2 hrs

2 onions, diced

2 cloves garlic, crushed

2 x 440g canned tomatoes

2 red capsicums, diced

2 x 440g canned red kidney
beans, rinsed, drained

2 carrots, diced

250g green beans, cut into
2cm pieces

½ cup tomato juice

¼ teaspoon chilli powder

¼ teaspoon smoked paprika

¼ teaspoon dill seeds

2 teaspoons finely grated
lemon rind

½ cup chopped fresh parsley

1 Heat slow cooker on high for 5 minutes.
Add onion, garlic and tomatoes and cook
for 25 minutes or until onion is soft.

2 Add all other ingredients except
parsley and cook on high for 1½ hours
until mixture combines and thickens.
Stir in parsley and serve.

Slow Vegetable Misto

serves 4

# Slow Vegetable Misto

**PREPARATION** 15 mins   **COOKING** 6 hrs

5 sticks celery, cut into 25mm pieces

12 baby carrots, cut in half lengthwise

2 medium onions, thinly sliced

200g fresh green beans

2 green capsicums, cubed

8 baby potatoes

400g canned chopped tomatoes

80g butter

2 tablespoons tapioca

pinch sugar

2 teaspoons salt

¼ teaspoon white pepper

1 tablespoon finely grated lemon rind

chopped fresh parsley to garnish

1  Place all vegetables except tomatoes and potatoes in a slow cooker set on low.

2  Combine tomatoes, butter, tapioca, sugar, salt and pepper and lemon rind. Pour over vegetables and stir well. Cover and cook on low for 3 hours or until vegetables are just tender.

3  Add the potatoes and cook for a further 3 hours. Adjust seasoning.

4  Serve topped with flat-leaf parsley and accompanied by fresh crusty bread.

West Indian Sweet Potato Risotto with Spiced Sour Cream

serves 6

# West Indian Sweet Potato Risotto with Spiced Sour Cream

**PREPARATION** 30 mins   **COOKING** 1 hr 45 mins

400g arborio rice

2 tablespoons olive oil

1 cup dry white wine

2 bay leaves

3 cups chicken stock

900g sweet potato

450g butternut pumpkin

2 onions, finely chopped

1 carrot, finely chopped

2 sticks celery, finely chopped

2 cloves garlic, crushed

1 teaspoon green curry paste

½ cup sour cream

¼ teaspoon ground cinnamon

¼ teaspoon ground coriander

¼ teaspoon ground cumin

½ bunch fresh chives, finely chopped

1   Add the rice and half of the olive oil to a slow cooker set on a high heat setting and stir to coat, making sure all the grains have a shiny surface. Add the wine and the bay leaves, and half of the stock. Stir the risotto, cover and cook for 45 minutes.

2   Meanwhile, peel and chop the sweet potato and pumpkin, reserving 200g of each and slicing it into matchsticks for later. Place the remainder in a saucepan and cover with water. Bring to the boil and simmer for 30 minutes until both vegetables are tender. Drain, then mash and add to the slow cooker with the remaining stock.

3   In a large saucepan, heat the remaining oil. Add the onions, carrot, celery, garlic, curry paste and reserved raw pumpkin and sweet potato, and sauté for 10 minutes until softened. Add to the slow cooker and stir to combine. Cook for a further hour or until all liquid is absorbed.

4   In a small bowl, whisk the sour cream with the spices. To serve, remove the bay leaves from the risotto, then mound the risotto in individual bowls and garnish with a generous dollop of spiced cream and a shower of chopped chives.

# Moroccan Potato and Lemon Casserole

serves 4

**PREPARATION** 20 mins   **COOKING** 3 hrs 35 mins

¼ cup olive oil

2 onions, sliced

3 cloves garlic, chopped

2 red chillies, finely chopped

1 teaspoon ground cumin

1 teaspoon ground coriander

900g kipfler potatoes, cut into 5mm slices

grated rind and juice of 1 lemon

3 cups vegetable stock

salt and freshly ground black pepper

⅓ cup sour cream

¼ cup chopped fresh parsley to garnish

1  Heat the oil in a frying pan. Add the onions, garlic, chillies, cumin and coriander, then gently fry for 2 minutes to release their flavours.

2  Stir in the potatoes, lemon rind and lemon juice to taste. Transfer to slow cooker on high and add the stock and seasoning. Cover and cook for 3½ hours or until the vegetables are tender and the liquid has reduced slightly.

3  Transfer to plates and top each serving with a spoonful of sour cream. Sprinkle over freshly chopped parsley to garnish.

serves 4–6

# Black Rice Pudding

**PREPARATION** 3 mins  **COOKING** 1 hr

1½ cups black glutinous rice

4–4½ cups water

1 pandan leaf

½ cup palm sugar syrup
(see below)

## PALM SUGAR SYRUP

1 cup grated palm sugar or
brown sugar

½ cup water

1  Rinse rice under cold running water for 1–2 minutes or until water is clear.

2  Combine rice, water and pandan leaf in a small slow cooker set on high and cook for 1 hour.

3  Meanwhile, to make syrup combine sugar and water in a small saucepan. Bring to the boil and simmer for 8 minutes. Then add to slow cooker and stir.

4  Serve pudding with coconut milk or ice cream.

**NOTE** Pandan leaves can be purchased fresh or frozen in most Asian supermarkets.

serves 6

# Montego Bananas

**PREPARATION** 10 mins   **COOKING** 2 hrs

12 bananas, sliced

2 vanilla beans, cut lengthwise

180g butter

⅔ cup coconut milk

2½ cups packed brown sugar

1 cup rum

1 teaspoon ground cinnamon

1 teaspoon ground nutmeg

1 cup pecans

½ cup shredded coconut

1 Layer sliced bananas and vanilla over base of a slow cooker.

2 Warm the butter and coconut milk in a small pot until butter melts, then in a small bowl combine with brown sugar, rum and spices. Ladle the mixture over the bananas. Cover and cook on high for 2 hours.

3 Cover the bananas with the pecans and coconut for the last 30 minutes of cooking, adding a little extra water if necessary.

serves 6

# Fruited Lebanese Semolina

**PREPARATION** 2 mins plus 15 mins soaking   **COOKING** 2 hrs

200g dried figs, quartered

100g dried apricots, sliced

100g pitted dried dates, sliced

60g prunes

30g currants

30g dried orange peel

1½ cups water

½ teaspoon ground cinnamon

½ cup semolina

1 tablespoon honey

⅛ teaspoon rose water

40g soft butter

## TOPPING

⅓ cup Greek-style yoghurt

4 mint leaves, sliced thinly

2 tablespoons flaked almonds, lightly toasted

6 sprigs mint to garnish

1   Combine dried fruits, half of the water and the cinnamon in a bowl. Stir to combine. Leave to soak for at least 15 minutes and stir again. Add the remaining water and all remaining ingredients to the fruit mixture.

2   Choose 6 moulds small enough to fit into the base of your slow cooker. Liberally coat the inside of moulds with butter and put into refrigerator to set, before adding the semolina mixture.

3   Divide mixture evenly between the prepared moulds, filling four-fifths of each mould. Place into the bottom of a large slow cooker and slowly add enough water around the moulds to come half way up the sides. Cook on a high heat setting for 2 hours.

4   Serve warm or refrigerate and serve chilled if desired. Serve topped with minted Greek-style yoghurt and toasted flaked almonds. Finish with a sprig of mint.

serves 6

# Spiced Fruit Compote

PREPARATION 2 mins    COOKING 2hrs 10 mins plus 20 mins cooling

750g mixed dried fruit

4½ cups water

⅔ cup slivered almonds

1 cinnamon stick

¼ teaspoon mixed spice

4 lemon slices

40g butter

2 tablespoons honey

¼ cup brandy

1  Heat a slow cooker on high and add all ingredients except the butter, honey and brandy. Cook for 2 hours.

2  After 2 hours remove ½ cup of liquid from the slow cooker (leaving all of the fruit behind). Add liquid to a saucepan with the butter, honey and brandy. Bring the liquid to the boil and continue to boil until it has reduced by half and formed a syrup. Pour back over the fruit and stir.

3  Turn cooker off and leave to cool slowly. The compote may be served warm, at room temperature, or chilled if desired. Serve with yoghurt or coconut rice (see page 179).

Coconut Rice

serves 4–6

# Coconut Rice

**PREPARATION** 2 mins   **COOKING** 8 hrs

600mL milk

600mL coconut milk

125g arborio rice

60g palm sugar, grated

1 Place all ingredients in a slow cooker and stir with a wooden spoon until combined.

2 Cook on a low setting for 8 hours. Serve with stewed brandy fruit pears (see page 183) or for breakfast serve with spiced fruit compote (see page 177).

Soft Baked Quinces

serves 4

# Soft Baked Quinces

**PREPARATION** 4 mins   **COOKING** 3 hrs 35 mins

4 medium-sized quinces,
cut in half, cored

50g butter

2 tablespoons honey

2 tablespoons brown sugar

½ cup dry red wine

½ cup water

⅓ cup toasted flaked almonds

4 tablespoons pure cream

1　Place quince halves in a slow cooker set on high.

2　Combine butter, honey, brown sugar, wine and water in a saucepan. Stir over low heat until sugar dissolves. Pour mixture over quinces.

3　Cover and cook for 3½ hours or until quinces are soft and bright red, basting the fruit twice near the end of the cooking time.

4　Serve quinces with almonds and pure cream.

Stewed Brandy Fruit Pears

serves 6

# Stewed Brandy Fruit Pears

**PREPARATION** 8 mins   **COOKING** 4 hrs 15 mins

6 pears

2 oranges, sliced

½ cup raisins

½ cup dried apricots, halved

1 cup water

½ cup brandy

60g butter

¾ cup brown sugar

¼ cup whole blanched almonds, roughly chopped

1 Cut a slice from the base of each pear so they sit flat.

2 Arrange pears, orange slices, raisins and apricots in a slow cooker.

3 Warm the water, brandy and butter together until butter melts, then combine with the brown sugar and pour over the fruits, covering orange slices well.

4 Cook for 3½ hours on low then add almonds. Cook for a further 45 minutes. Serve warm, with coconut rice if desired (see page 179).

**NOTE** You can replace the brandy with orange juice if you want to make this a breakfast dish.

Slow-Cooked Dates and Apples

serves 8

# Slow-Cooked Dates and Apples

**PREPARATION** 10 mins   **COOKING** 2 hrs

10 large green apples, peeled and sliced

400g fresh dates, stoned, halved

2 cups apple juice

juice of 1 lemon

finely grated rind of 2 oranges

juice of 4 oranges

3 cinnamon sticks

½ cup honey

Greek yoghurt to serve

ground cinnamon to garnish

1 Place the apple slices in a slow cooker. Stir in the dates, juices, rind and cinnamon sticks. Drizzle the honey over the mixture. Cover and cook on low for 2 hours until the apples only just hold their shape.

2 Serve warm or chilled with Greek yoghurt, dusted with cinnamon.

Peaches in Pink Wine

serves 4

# Peaches in Pink Wine

**PREPARATION** 2 mins   **COOKING** 1 hr 30 mins plus 30 mins cooling

4 ripe peaches, halved,
stones removed

3 cups rosé (pink wine)

½ cup caster sugar

1 cinnamon stick

1  Place peaches in a large bowl. Cover with boiling water and leave for 30–60 seconds. Using a slotted spoon, remove peaches from boiling water and run under cold water. Remove skins and transfer peaches to a slow cooker.

2  Add wine, sugar and cinnamon stick and cook on high for 1½ hours. Place in the refrigerator to cool.

3  Serve peaches cold with syrup.

Indian Rice Pudding with Pistachios

serves 4

# Indian Rice Pudding with Pistachios

**PREPARATION** 5 mins   **COOKING** 2 hrs 10 mins

60g basmati rice

1½ cups milk

375mL evaporated milk

3 cardamom pods, bruised

1 cinnamon stick

60g caster sugar

2 tablespoons flaked almonds, toasted

30g shelled pistachios, roughly chopped

1 Place the rice, milk and evaporated milk in a small heavy-based saucepan and bring to a simmer, taking care not to let the mixture boil. Simmer, uncovered, for 10 minutes. While mixture is cooking, heat slow cooker on a high heat setting.

2 Transfer the rice mixture to slow cooker, then stir in the cardamom, cinnamon, sugar and nuts, reserving 1 tablespoon of pistachios to garnish. Cover and cook for 2 hours or until reaching a thick consistency. Remove the cinnamon stick. Serve warm or cold, garnished with the reserved pistachios.

# Index

We are proud to present the **COLLECTORS EDITION** series of books as a suite of our favourite and most asked for recipes.

This series is bound together in a premium collectable format that can be added to the recipe section of your bookshelf.

Watch out for the following titles, start collecting, continue cooking, and finally, enjoy the end results of a beautifully prepared meal.